NUREG-1744

Assessment of the TRAC-M Codes Using Flecht-Seaset Reflood and Steam Cooling Data

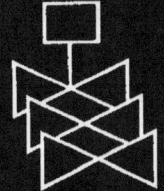

U.S. Nuclear Regulatory Commission
Office Nuclear Regulatory Research
Washington, DC 20555-0001

AVAILABILITY OF REFERENCE MATERIALS
IN NRC PUBLICATIONS

NUREG-1744

Assessment of the TRAC-M Codes Using Flecht-Seaset Reflood and Steam Cooling Data

Manuscript Completed: May 2001
Date Published: May 2001

Prepared by
F. Odar

Division of Systems Analysis and Regulatory Effectiveness
Office of Nuclear Regulatory Research
U.S. Nuclear Regulatory Commission
Washington, DC 20555-0001

ABSTRACT

This report presents the results of an assessment of the capabilities of the TRAC-M(F77), Version 5.5.2.A, and TRAC-M(F90), Version 3.580, codes to predict reflood and steam cooling phenomena that may occur during a postulated large-break loss-of-coolant accident (LOCA). The assessment is predicated on test data from Flecht-Seaset Runs 31504 and 32753. The assessment shows that predictions of the reflood phenomena derived using both codes are inaccurate; however, it is judged that they can conservatively predict peak clad temperatures in heated rods since the code model expels more water from the test section than measured. The predictions of steam cooling in single-phase flow conditions are acceptable.

TABLE OF CONTENTS

FIGURES

EXECUTIVE SUMMARY

This report presents an assessment of the capabilities of the TRAC-M(F77), Version 5.5.2.A, and TRAC-M(F90), Version 3.580, codes to predict reflood and steam cooling phenomena for pressurized water reactors during a large-break loss-of-coolant accident. The assessment of the reflood predictive capability is performed using test data from Flecht-Seaset Run 31504, while the assessment of steam cooling is performed using test data from Flecht-Seaset Run 32753. These tests simulate unblocked bundle forced reflood and steam cooling conditions in PWRs.

The top-level requirement in the development of a thermal-hydraulic code is that the code should correctly model the physics of the phenomena. This assessment shows that both TRAC codes fail to correctly model flow regime maps during reflood and, consequently, they do not correctly predict interfacial areas between phases, vapor fractions, phasic velocities, and temperatures. Almost none of the important parameters (such as clad temperatures, steam temperatures, differential pressures, and liquid and steam carryouts) are consistently predicted throughout the range within the acceptable accuracy. The predictions in ranges where clad temperatures are predicted within accuracy limits are accidental. The model in the codes predict higher liquid carryout than measured in the test. This would indicate that the codes will predict higher clad temperatures than measured in the test data, thereby yielding conservative predictions.

The Office of Nuclear Regulatory Research has a research program in place at Pennsylvania State University (PSU) to improve the agency's capability to model reflood phenomena using its system analysis codes. The findings in this report provide guidance on how future modeling of reflood should proceed. This report assesses the code against one particular Flecht-Seaset (F-S) run. However, the decision to initiate the PSU test program was based on several reflood cases at various facilities. These cases exhibit the overall trend that TRAC-M(F90) overpredicts peak clad temperature (PCT), even though the predictions are in reasonable agreement with runs made at the CCTF and SCTF facilities. The TRAC-P code series has been used by NRC to perform LOCA analysis because of this conservative trend. However, as the agency begins to risk-inform its regulations, new designs are submitted and licensees request further uprates. NRC would be better equipped to audit licensee submittals with a less conservative, more accurate reflood model. In order to model reflood accurately for all designs, conditions and test facilities, the proper physics must be modeled mechanistically. The author recommends that new flow regime maps for reflood be constructed and the selection criteria for the maps should also include effects of both phasic velocities.

The assessment with the steam cooling test data shows that both TRAC-M codes correctly predict the single-phase convective flow heat transfer with acceptable accuracy. The agreement between predictions and the test data is "Excellent" to "Reasonable." It is judged that "Excellent" agreement throughout the whole region of valid testing may be obtained by modeling the input deck in more detail.

SECTION 1

INTRODUCTION

This report presents the results of an assessment of the capabilities of the TRAC-M(F90), Version 3.580, and TRAC-M(F77), Version 5.5.2A, codes to calculate reflood and steam cooling phenomena for pressurized-water reactors (PWRs). The reflood assessment was performed using test data from Flecht-Seaset Run 31504, while the steam cooling assessment was performed using test data from Flecht-Seaset Run 32753. These tests simulate unblocked bundle forced reflood and steam cooling conditions in PWRs.

Section 2 of this report discusses the reflood phenomenon and requirements for the code's predictive capabilities. It begins by discussing the reflood phenomena, in general, as they would occur in a PWR during a postulated large-break loss-of-coolant accident (LOCA). It then discusses what part of the reflood phenomena would be simulated in Flecht-Seaset tests. Finally, it discusses the requirements that are necessary for thermal-hydraulic codes to predict the reflood phenomena.

Section 3 of this report describes the configuration of the Flecht-Seaset facility and the test procedures that are used to conduct reflood and steam cooling tests. It then describes the heater bundle and various system components, as well as the instrumentation that is used in the system.

Section 4 describes the results of the assessment that was performed using Flecht-Seaset Run 31504. This section assesses the capabilities of the TRAC-M(F77) and TRAC-M(F90) codes to predict reflood phenomena. It begins by describing the success metrics and expected uncertainties. Next, it compares calculations with the actual test data, reviews important aspects of the various code models that are used in modeling reflood phenomena, and presents conclusions on the basis of the requirements presented in Section 2.

Section 5 describes the results of the assessment that was performed using Flecht-Seaset Run 32753. This section assesses the capabilities of the TRAC-M(F77) and TRAC-M(F90) codes to predict steam cooling phenomena. It begins by describing the success metrics and expected uncertainties. Next, it compares calculations with the actual test data, and presents conclusions.

SECTION 2

REFLOOD PHENOMENA AND CODE REQUIREMENTS

2.1 Description of the Phenomena

The purpose of reflooding the core is to protect the integrity of the fuel cladding. During a large-break LOCA, cladding temperature changes as follows:

- Cladding temperature increases during blowdown from normal operating conditions of approximately 325°C to approximately 550–800°C (roughly 1000–1500°F).

- During refill and reflood, cladding temperature varies because of the decay heat generation in fuel rods and heat removal by two-phase flow through the core. Cladding temperature increases as long as heat removal is less than heat generation. Cladding temperature decreases when heat removal is greater than heat generation.

- As reflood progresses, the cladding very rapidly quenches and cools to the saturation temperature as the cladding surface becomes wetted.

The emergency core cooling (ECC) systems are designed to inject water into the primary system, and to recover or reflood a potentially uncovered core. Steam produced during the core quenching process creates a pressure that is balanced against the hydraulic height difference between the core and the downcomer. The pressure differential is limited by the height of the cold leg.

As the reflood water enters the core, it is heated by the stored energy and decay power of the rods. Depending on the time during the transient and injection flow rate, the reflood water at the quench front can be subcooled or saturated, or the water can reach saturation below the quench front so that a two-phase mixture reaches the quench front. During the reflood, the hydraulic conditions on the rod surfaces change completely from unwetted to wetted conditions within a few seconds. At the quench front, the stored energy of the rod is released over a relatively short distance in which the local axial temperature gradient can be as large as 500 K/cm. The transition boiling heat transfer regime exists during these few seconds. Correct modeling of the transition boiling is important in order to accurately predict core reflood behavior.

A high heat flux over a short rod length is a very significant aspect of the reflood process. Figure 2.1 illustrates the variation in the rod temperature during a reflood test, along with the calculated surface heat flux obtained from the Semiscale Mod-3 test data (Ref. 1). During the 1-second time period around 59 s, a large heat flux occurs as the rod returns to a wetted nucleate boiling condition. This would imply the occurrence of critical heat flux (CHF) at 59 s, i.e., at t_2. Quenching starts slightly earlier, at t_1. The rod surface temperature at this time is at the quench temperature, T_q where the direct contact between the liquid and the wall starts.

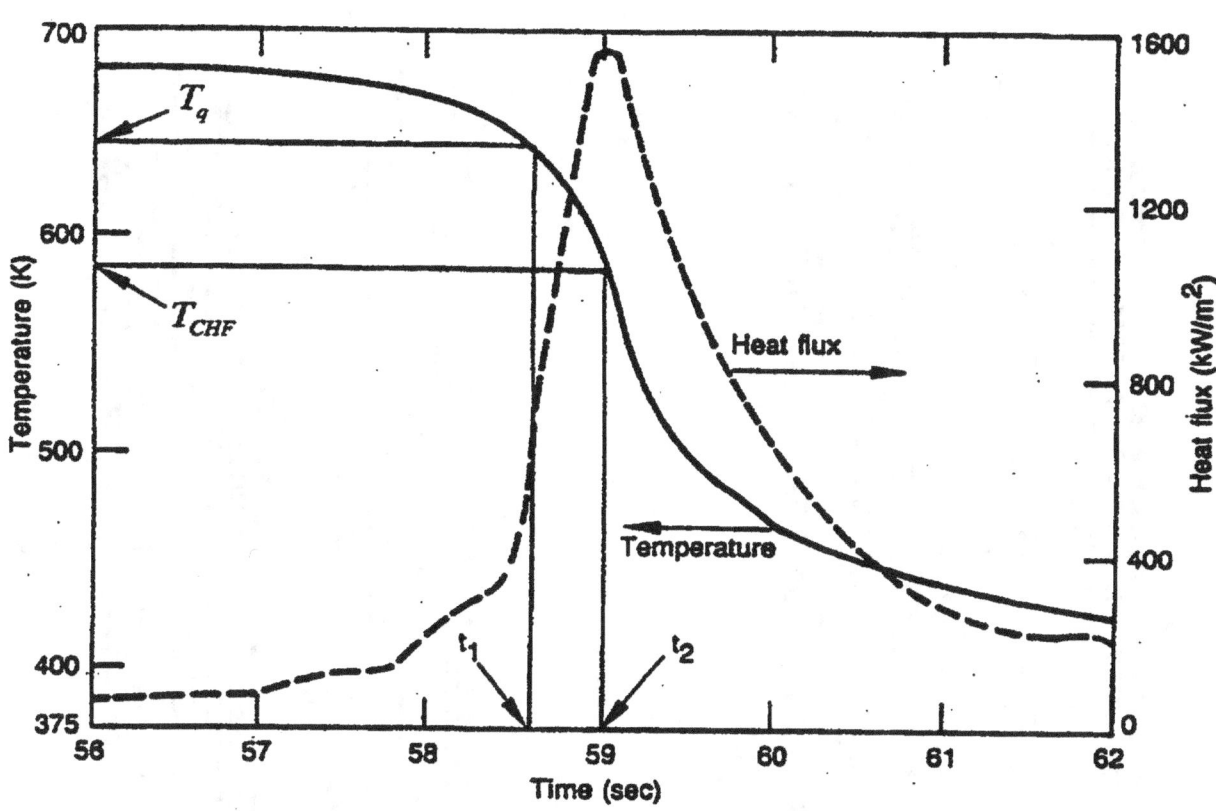

Figure 2.1 Sketch of Transition Boiling During Reflood

The transition boiling region starts at t_1 and ends at t_2. In the transition boiling region after t_1, as the frequency and duration of direct contact between the liquid and the wall increase, the heat flux increases; and consequently, the rod surface temperature decreases.

Based on the flooding rate and subcooling and quality of the incoming fluid various flow regimes may appear during a reflood. Figure 2.2 illustrates sketches of flow patterns observed in reflood tests with saturated and subcooled inlet conditions. Saturated conditions are associated with low inlet flows, about 1.0-in/s (0.0254m/s). In the case of a reflood with saturated low inlet flow, the vapor generated at the quench front sputters and causes a transition from an annular to a frothy flow regime followed by Dispersed-Flow Film Boiling, DFFB, regime. Details of the frothy regime will be discussed in Section 2.3.1. The steam generation from quenching produces very large vapor velocities which entrain and shear liquid filaments into droplets. During this process, the vapor fraction changes from low to moderate. These droplets are then swept into the upper region of the core producing dispersed flow film boiling. The cooling produced by these droplets is called "precursory cooling." During a large break LOCA this is the prevailing flow pattern during reflood since the incoming fluid flow to the inlet of the core, after the refill process is over, is usually saturated or close to saturation and the flow rates are generally low.

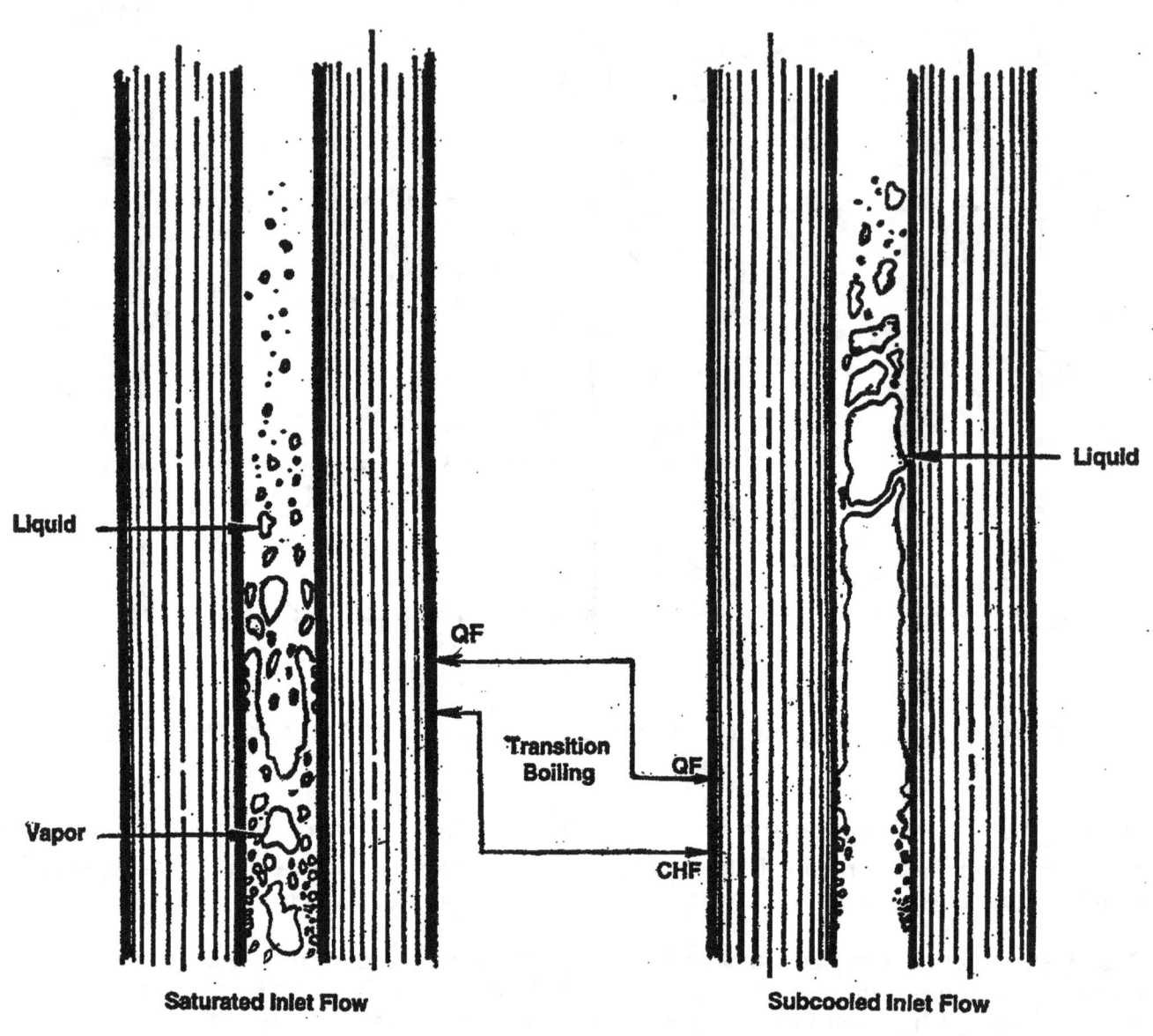

Figure 2.2 Flow Patterns During Reflood

At high inlet flows, about 6.0-in/s (0.15-m/s), with high subcooling, a different flow pattern emerges as the right sketch of Figure 2.2 illustrates. An Inverted-Annular Film Boiling, IAFB, takes place immediately downstream of the quench front. Just above the quench front, a stable film boiling regime develops. The flow pattern is characterized by a single-phase liquid core. At this location, the quality of the two-phase fluid is considered low. This implies that the liquid is still subcooled and most of the heat from the rods is absorbed by raising the liquid temperature. Further downstream, the liquid core is still surrounded by the vapor annulus and it is hydrodynamically unstable, Ref. 2. Heat transfer rates across the vapor film will vary greatly with surface wave motion at the vapor liquid interface. Further along the channel an unstable flow pattern transition regime develops resulting in a dispersed flow. Generally, heat transfer rates are high and the quench front quickly propagates up the bundle. During a large break LOCA, this type of flow pattern does not occur too often since the incoming flow to the inlet of the core is generally not subcooled and the flow rates are not very high.

During a reflood, steam is mainly generated at the quench front, causing entrainment of water slugs, fragments, and droplets upward through the core. Knowledge of the extent of entrainment is necessary to predict the hydrodynamic and thermal response in the core. If the steam velocity exceeds a certain value, entrained water can be swept completely out of the core. At lower velocities, partial entrainment and levitation of the water may occur. As the entrained water travels upward through the core, water fragments and droplets impact the rod walls and cause local cooling. Entrained liquid also absorbs heat by radiation from the rods and by convection from superheated steam. Thermal non-equilibrium may exist with saturated water droplets and superheated steam. Therefore, there is a complex heat transfer process from cladding to steam and from steam to droplet where evaporation of the droplet can occur. In addition, there is a gradient of steam temperature from the quench front where mostly saturated conditions exist (with moderate qualities) to the top of the core where there is a high-quality mixture with high superheat.

The heat transfer mechanism in this dispersed flow region is the most important mechanism during the reflood. After the blowdown before the reflood, the reactor core experiences an almost adiabatic heat-up. As the water enters the core, water droplets produced by liquid entrainment and fragmentation contact the hot rods and begin core cooling. Rod temperatures attain their maximum values, and then turn around.

Spacer grids are structural members in the reactor core that support the fuel rods at a predetermined rod-to-rod pitch. All fuel assemblies have grid spacers at the same elevation across the core. Since the grid represents a perturbation to the flow channel, its thermal-hydraulic effects are important. The grid reduces the fuel assembly flow area by contracting the flow and then expanding it downstream of each grid. During normal operation, the flow is single-phase liquid. The flow contracts and accelerates within the grid and then expands downstream, thereby disrupting and reestablishing the fluid and thermal boundary layers on the fuel rod. This mechanism increases the local heat transfer within and downstream of the grid. Several single-phase experiments have shown that the single-phase heat transfer downstream of a grid spacer can be modeled as an entrance effect phenomenon in which the abrupt contraction and expansion result in the establishment of a new boundary layer downstream of the grid. During a large-break LOCA, the flow is no longer single-phase, and the thermal/hydraulic effects of the grid spacer must be evaluated in terms of two-phase flow.

During reflood, grid spacers interact with the fuel rods and the two-phase flow in the flow channels. From various two-phase flow studies, it has been observed that grid spacers caused enhancement of the heat transfer, mainly by desuperheating the vapor. The enhancement of heat transfer results from three mechanisms:

(1) grid rewet
(2) convective enhancement
(3) droplet breakup

Since the grids are unpowered, they can quench before the fuel rods. If the grids rewet, they create additional liquid surface area that can help to desuperheat the vapor in the non-equilibrium two-phase droplet flow. The region surrounding a wetted grid will have a higher interfacial heat transfer coefficient (compared to droplets) because the velocity for the vapor flow relative to the liquid film is larger. In addition to desuperheating the vapor, the liquid film will evaporate, resulting in higher steam flow and convective heat transfer. The increased interfacial heat transfer between the film on the grid and the vapor flow and the generation of additional saturated vapor from the liquid film on the grid will result in lower vapor temperatures downstream of the grids. In addition, the grids can also break up the entrained droplets into smaller ones, thereby increasing the surface area for evaporation. The evaporation of the smaller droplets will provide an additional steam source which increases the convective heat transfer coefficient.

Thermal-hydraulic processes in a reactor during normal operation are basically one-dimensional. During the blowdown portion of a large-break LOCA, the process is one-dimensional. During reflood, multidimensional flow patterns occur in the vessel core and upper plenum for the following reasons:

- Nonuniformities in core power distribution, intermittent positioning of the primary loops circumferentially around the vessel, and differences in resistance to flow through the intact and broken hot legs naturally tend to promote multidimensional effects.

- As the flow passes through the upper plenum, it must flow around several structural elements. Furthermore, the flow behavior of a collected pool in the upper plenum may be highly three-dimensional because of the tendency of the water pool to collect in dead spaces and in regions near walls and structures and in certain portions of the upper plenum as a result of the flow pattern toward the hot legs

Liquid deentrainment occurs when water entrained in the steam is removed from the steam flow at other places in the core, the upper plenum, or beyond. Deentrainment occurs as a result of gravitational or inertial forces. Deentrainment is enhanced when the flow slows down because of a flow area increase, or when the flow changes direction to pass around obstructions or structures or to turn out through a nozzle. This deentrainment removes entrained water from the two-phase flow mixture, and deentrained water that accumulates in the core and upper plenum provides a source of water for core cooling that supplements the cooling obtained by bottom reflood. This enhances core cooling near the fuel assembly grid spacers, and is also important for the upper regions of the core.

The extent of a liquid carryover to the upper plenum is expressed by the liquid carryover rate fraction; that is, the ratio of a total liquid mass flow rate out of the core to the liquid mass entering the core. A liquid carryover reduces the rate of accumulation of water within the core, and provides a source of water for deentrainment in the upper plenum.

Pool formation refers to the collection or behavior of water in the upper plenum during reflood. The source of this water is entrained water carried up from the core, which is then deentrained in the upper plenum. The upper plenum contains a significant number of internal structures that act as a steam separator to deentrain liquid in the two-phase flow. In addition, the decrease in flow velocities from the core to the upper plenum allows gravitational separation of liquid from steam. The flow behavior of a collected pool may be highly three-dimensional because of the tendency of the water pool to collect in low-flow areas and in regions near the walls and structures. Upper plenum pool formation is important to LOCA/ECCS performance for the following reasons:

(1) The pool provides a source of additional cooling water for the core. Additionally deentrainment and pool formation reduce the carryover to the steam generator.

(2) The pool can reduce the flooding rate by creating a static head pressure drop in the upper plenum.

(3) Water flows downward from the upper plenum into the core under the influence of gravity. This downward flow is opposed by steam flow upward from the core. The downward flow tends to be nonuniform or channeled as a result of upward steam flow. The radial power profile in the core and the variations in stored heat developed by uneven quenching cause development of nonuniform upward steam flow.

Top-down quenching occurs when the top portions of the fuel rods quench before the portions just below. Top-down quenching provides additional cooling to the upper core and, in some cases, to the intermediate and/or lower core that primarily obtains the cooling from bottom reflood. In standard designs, top-down quenching may occur from the fallback of water that is deentrained at the top of the core or in the upper plenum. Different reactor designs (such as upper head injection and AP600) provide substantial top-down quench during reflood using different processes. This results in quenching of the uppermost part of the fuel rods sooner than would occur from the propagation of the bottom quench front. In standard designs, top-down cooling does not generally extend to the hot spot in the core, which is typically at about two-thirds of the core height.

Radial power distribution causes radial gradients in steam generation and liquid entrainment. Thermal-hydraulic effects resulting from radial power distributions are important because they lead to crossflows between the low-powered assemblies and the high-powered assemblies. The variations in the quench front elevation across the core yield a radial profile that resembles the inverse of the radial power profile (i.e., lower quench front elevation in higher-powered bundles and conversely). Radial variations in the vapor generation cause variations in the entrainment and liquid fraction above the quench front (i.e., greater entrainment in higher powered bundles). There is relatively free lateral communication in the core. Horizontal pressure differences and crossflows are established by the radial power distribution. The net effect is an increase in the water flow rate and cooling of the higher-powered bundles (assemblies) compared to the cooling given the average flow rate entering the bottom of the core. Such crossflows tend to prevent some hot spots from developing.

At the beginning of a reflood, a manometer-type oscillation can occur. The name derives from the general observation that the core and downcomer levels oscillate like the levels in a U-tube manometer that has been perturbed. The U-bend manometer is formed by the downcomer water column and the core water column, and is connected by the lower plenum. This phenomenon was observed in several facilities including the loss-of-fluid test (LOFT), Semiscale, slab core test facility (SCTF), cylindrical core test facility (CCTF), and full-length emergency core heat transfer (FLECHT). Manometer oscillations are initiated by the sudden rapid introduction of ECCS water into the core inlet associated with accumulator injection. As water penetrates into the core, rapid generation of steam occurs and pressure begins to build up in the upper portion of the core. This tends to push water from the core into the downcomer. As the core water level goes down, the steam generation rate and the back-pressure are reduced. This reduced pressure, in conjunction with the increased downcomer level, causes a reversal and the core level rises again. The subsequent upward movement of the core level tends to overshoot the equilibrium location, leading again to increased steam generation. This causes an oscillatory movement of both the collapsed core water level and the downcomer level. The importance of manometer oscillations is a potential increase or decrease in the core cooling rate, depending upon which cycle of the oscillation the core is in. The increased cooling rate is caused by more rod surface area being covered with water during the upward surge of the oscillations. The decreased cooling occurs when the collapsed water level in the core is low.

As ECC water enters the hot core, some of it will turn into steam. The resulting increase in pressure tends to suppress the reflooding velocity in the core. This retarding effect of steam on the reflood rate is referred to as "steam binding." Another source of back-pressure retarding the ECC injection rate is liquid carried to the steam generators and evaporated as a result of heat transfer from the secondary side to the primary side. Finally, the steam binding effect may occur as a result of the leakage of hot secondary liquid to the primary side through a concurrent steam generator tube rupture.

In Babcock & Wilcox reactor designs, eight check valves are located in the core barrel between the upper plenum and the downcomer annulus above the inlet nozzles. These valves are held shut during normal reactor operation by the discharge pressure from the reactor coolant pumps. In the event of a LOCA, the vent valves open during the refill, and steam flows through the vent valves to the ECCS-induced condensation point in the downcomer annulus. During the reflood, steam generated in the core flows through the vent valves to the system break and, thus, bypasses the loop flow resistance. This relieves the steam pressure above the core, and allows an increased reflood rate.

Appendix K to 10 CFR Part 50 requires that any effect of a fuel rod flow blockage must be explicitly accounted for in safety analysis calculations when the core reflood rate drops below 1.0 in/s. The effect of a flow blockage on heat transfer is a combination of two competing thermal-hydraulic phenomena. Specifically, flow area reduction causes flow acceleration, droplet breakup, improved mixing, and steam desuperheating, and consequently increased heat removal rates. In addition, flow bypass reduces the flow rate through the blocked region. These two effects are dependent on blockage geometry and distribution.

2.2 Predictive Models and Experimental Facilities

As discussed in the previous section, many different phenomena are involved during a reflood process. Some of these phenomena occur because of different reactor designs. However, most of these phenomena occur in all designs because they are fundamental to the reflood process. Their dominance may be different in different reactors or different types of LOCAs. These phenomena are listed below:

1. bottom quench
2. liquid entrainment and precursor cooling
3. vapor superheat
4. heat transfer
5. liquid deentrainment
6. top-down quenching
7. radial power effects and three-dimensional flow
8. manometer oscillations
9. initial cladding temperature effects
10. liquid carryover from the core
11. upper plenum geometry effects and pool formation
12. liquid carryover to the hot leg
13. steam binding
14. grid spacer effects
15. flow blockage effects
16. vent valve effects

The models in thermal-hydraulic codes should be capable of predicting the above phenomena with acceptable accuracy. In most PWRs in the United States, the ECC is injected through cold legs, and passes down the downcomer into the lower plenum and up the core. Hence, "bottom reflood" of the core after a large-break LOCA is the predominant mode of quenching the core, and many experiments have been conducted to study the thermal-hydraulic phenomena of bottom reflood. Depending on the reflooding rate, different flow regimes may develop ahead of the quench front as the core is quenched from the bottom up. In most U.S.-designed reactors, the first 15 phenomena may occur during a postulated LOCA. In Babcock & Wilcox plant designs, the last phenomenon related to vent valve operation also becomes important.

Much of the U.S. database for reflood heat transfer comes from the PWR FLECHT and Full-Length Emergency Core Heat Transfer System Effects and Separate Effects (Flecht-Seaset) programs (Refs. 3 and 4). The Semiscale program has also produced a data set on core thermal-hydraulics of reflood (Refs. 5 and 6). In Japan, the earlier reflood experiments and extensive CCTF and SCTF tests by the Japan Atomic Energy Research Institute (JAERI) provide a database of large-scale test facilities. The Japanese CCTF and SCTF test facilities are the largest reflood test facilities in the world. Similar smaller reflood test facilities exist in France (Ref. 7), Germany (Refs. 8 and 9), and the United Kingdom (Ref. 10). There are also small-scale test facilities at several universities, such as the University of California at Los Angeles (UCLA) (Ref. 11), University of New York at Stony Brook (Ref. 12), and the University of California at Berkeley (Ref. 13). These small-scale university test facilities help to develop models and understanding that can help in interpreting the behavior and performance of the larger-scale tests.

2.3 Discussion of the Phenomena Observed in Flecht-Seaset Tests

This report presents assessment studies of the TRAC-M code using the data from the Flecht-Seaset facility performed using the 161-rod unblocked test section. This section discusses which of the phenomena listed in the previous section can be assessed using Flecht-Seaset testing. The Flecht-Seaset facility simulates only one-dimensional reflood phenomena. In the Flecht-Seaset program, visual observations could be made through view ports located at several elevations of the bundle. Since the hydraulics and heat transfer are closely coupled, the interactions among system parameters (such as flooding rate, pressure, subcooling, initial cladding temperature, and mass effluent fraction) have been studied. Among these parameters, the flooding rate was found to be the most influential. Different flooding rates gave rise to different flow regimes which, in turn, determined the increase in the cladding temperature and the quenching of the cores. A detailed analysis of the data was presented in Ref. 4, and the important observations and a description of the phenomena are summarized herein.

2.3.1 Bottom Quench, Transition Zone, Liquid Entrainment, Precursor Cooling, and Heat Transfer

Figures 2.3 and 2.4 illustrate the effect of variations in the flooding rate on the heat transfer coefficient and peak temperatures at the mid-plane elevation for some of the runs in the 161-rod bundle unblocked test section used in the Flecht-Seaset program. The figures show an orderly increase in heat transfer at all times as the flooding rate increases. Temperatures show a more rapid turnaround, and peak temperatures were lower as the flooding rate was increased.

Figures 2.5 and 2.6 show the quench front progress. As expected, the higher the flooding rate, the faster the quench front moves up. Figure 2.6 shows the trend of increasing temperatures with decreasing flooding rates. These trends are expected to occur.

For the low flooding rates, a transition zone, or a froth region exists above a quench front. In the transition zone the flow is not quite dispersed as shown in Fig. 2.2. Hence, the heat transfer mechanism in the transition zone differs from that in the dispersed flow and from that below the quench front. In order to apply the proper heat transfer mechanism when calculating heat transfer from the hot wall to the two-phase flow, knowledge of the length of this transition zone is required. Murao (Ref. 14) observed that temperature history curves during reflood show a sudden change to a steeper slope sometime before quench (see Period II in Figure 2.7). This slope change is related to the flow regime change ahead of the quench front. Similar behavior was observed in the FLECHT tests, and a method was developed to calculate the length of the transition zone above the quench front. It is possible to distinguish three different flow regimes as indicated in Figure 2.7. The first occurs when there is a dispersed droplet flow at the elevation (Period I), after a short period of single-phase steam flow. The second occurs when the transition zone above the quench front is at the elevation (Period II), and the third occurs when the quench front is above the elevation (Period III). These different flow regimes are distinguished in the heat transfer coefficient curves of Figure 2.7. The relatively moderate increases in heat transfer during Period I are followed by a rather sharp increase in heat transfer during Period II, and the quench produces a further sudden increase. It is observed that the transition zone could be about 0.3 m for a reflooding rate of 0.0254 m/s (1.0 in/s), and could increase to about 1 meter for a reflooding rate of 0.076 m/s. In these tests, the transition zone length is a direct function of the reflood rate. Figures 2.8 and 2.9 illustrate the progress of fronts relative to quench data for slow and fast reflood runs, respectively.

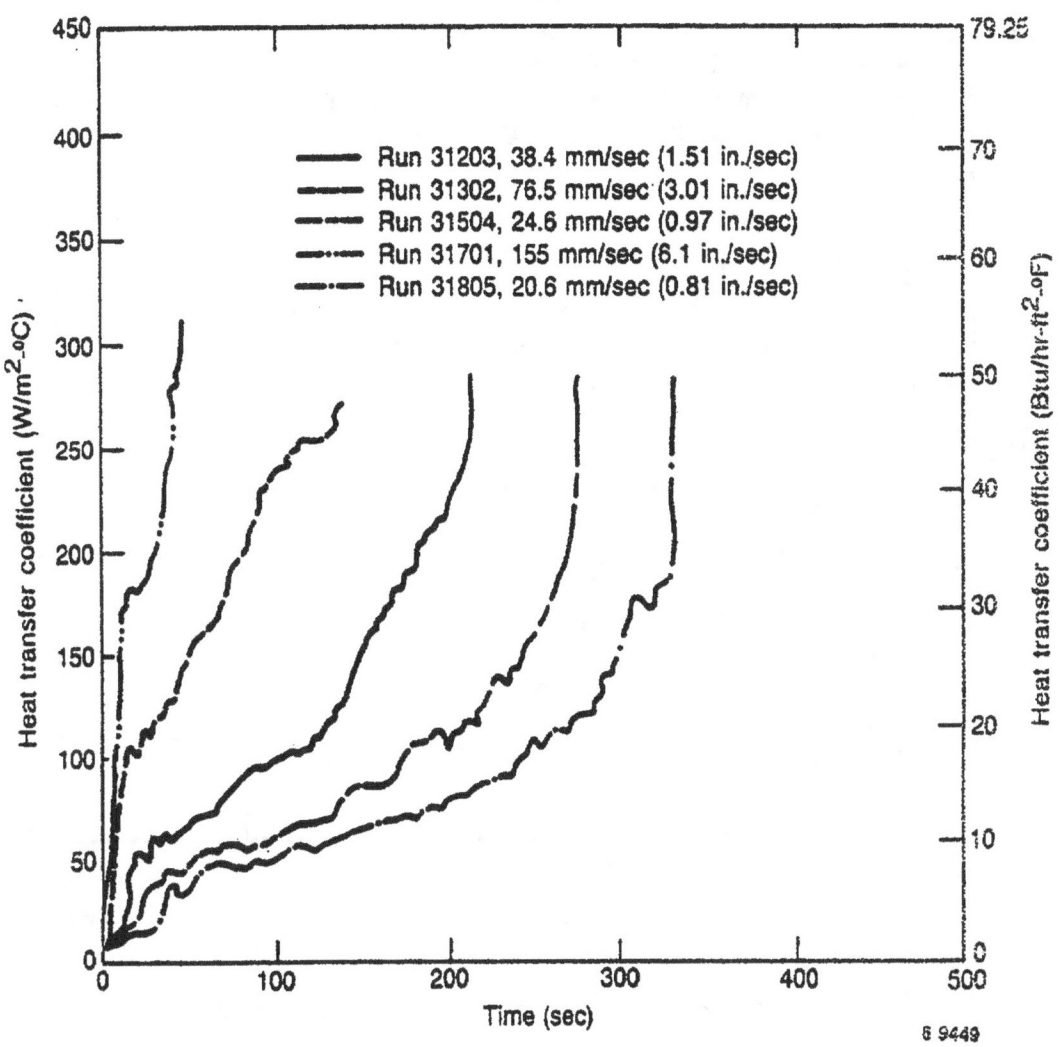

Figure 2.3 Flooding Rate vs Heat Transfer Coefficient

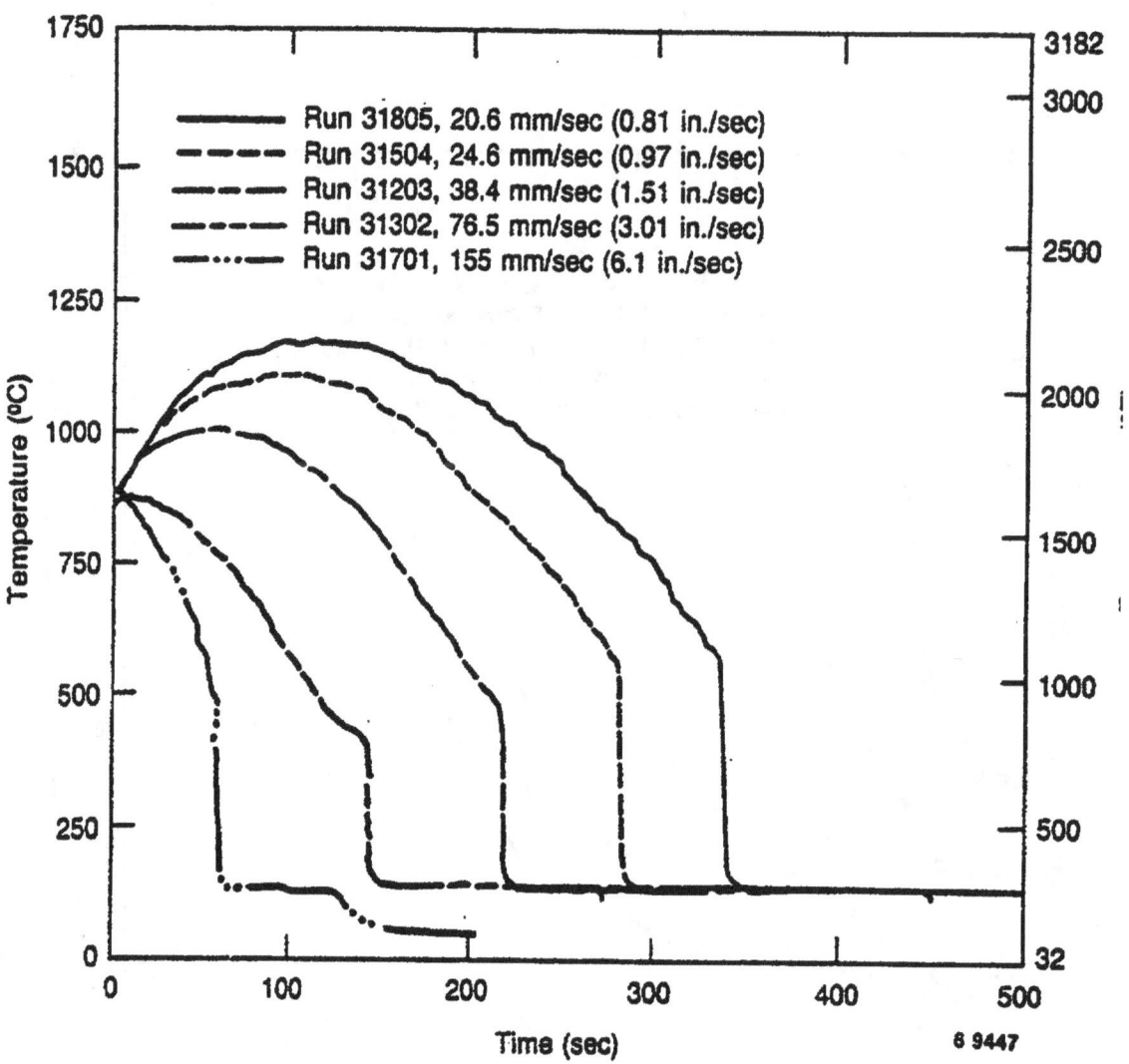

Figure 2.4 Flooding Rate vs Clad Temperatures

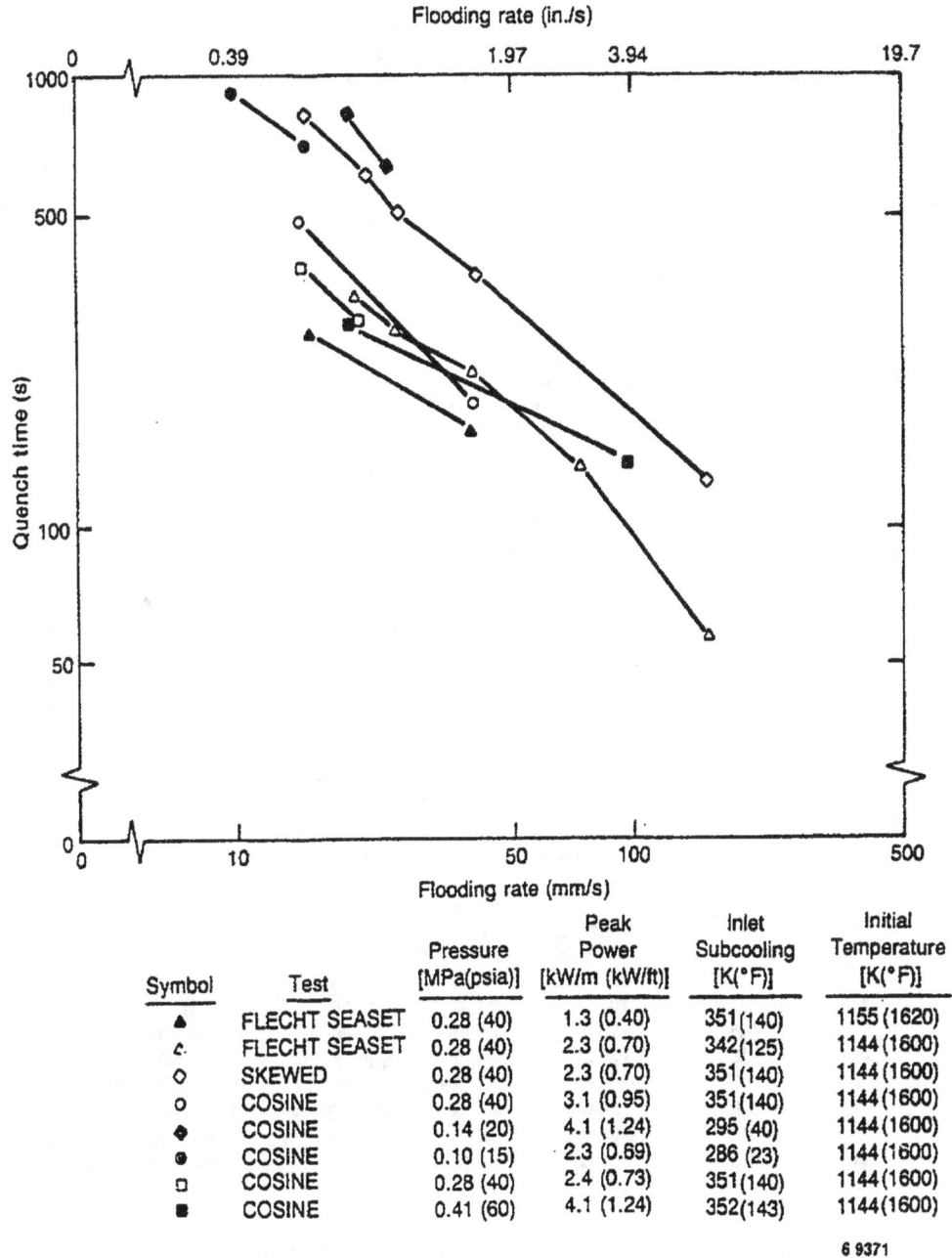

Symbol	Test	Pressure [MPa(psia)]	Peak Power [kW/m (kW/ft)]	Inlet Subcooling [K(°F)]	Initial Temperature [K(°F)]
▲	FLECHT SEASET	0.28 (40)	1.3 (0.40)	351 (140)	1155 (1620)
▵	FLECHT SEASET	0.28 (40)	2.3 (0.70)	342 (125)	1144 (1600)
◇	SKEWED	0.28 (40)	2.3 (0.70)	351 (140)	1144 (1600)
○	COSINE	0.28 (40)	3.1 (0.95)	351 (140)	1144 (1600)
◈	COSINE	0.14 (20)	4.1 (1.24)	295 (40)	1144 (1600)
◉	COSINE	0.10 (15)	2.3 (0.69)	286 (23)	1144 (1600)
□	COSINE	0.28 (40)	2.4 (0.73)	351 (140)	1144 (1600)
■	COSINE	0.41 (60)	4.1 (1.24)	352 (143)	1144 (1600)

6 9371

Figure 2.5 Flooding Rate vs. Quench Time

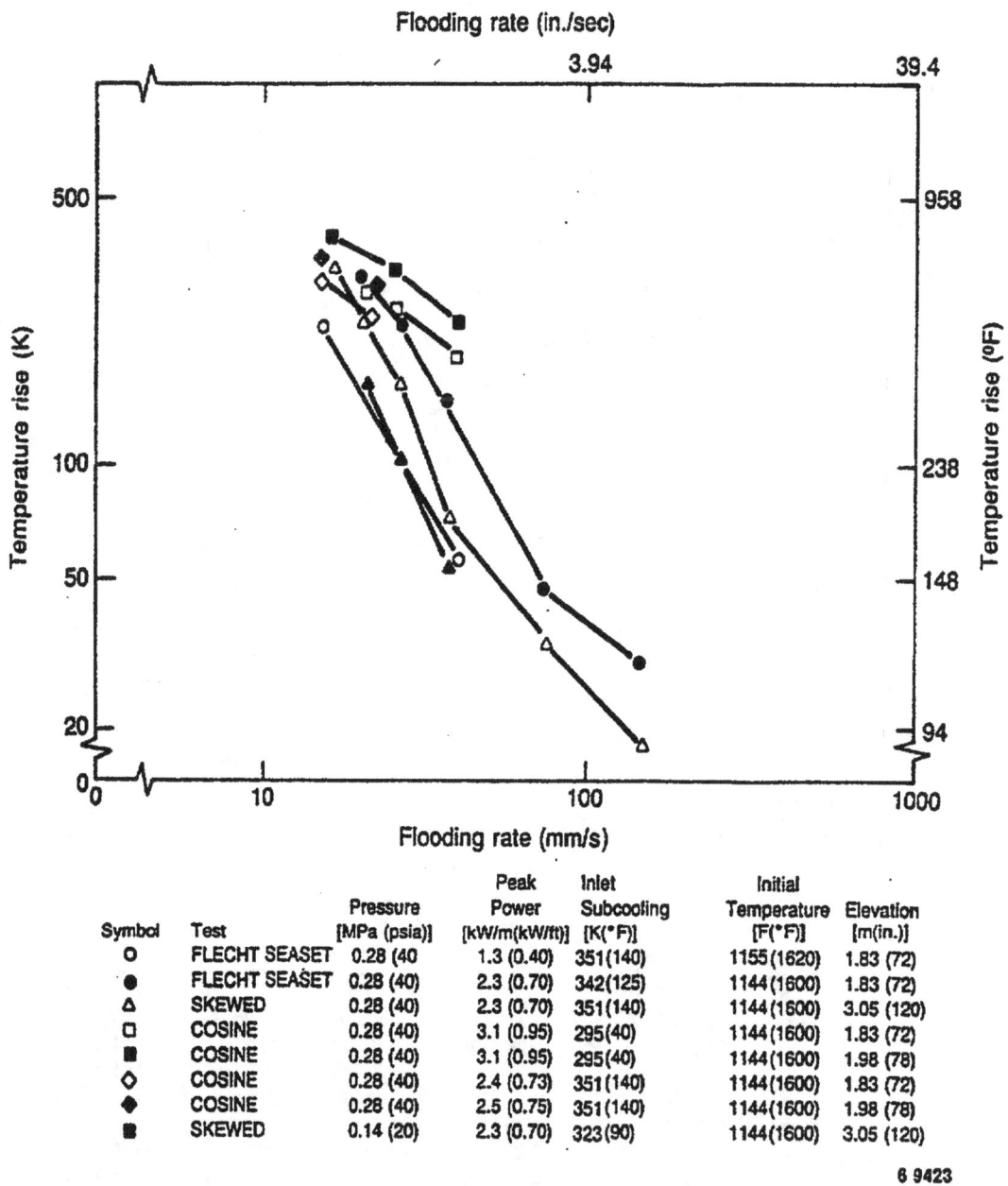

Symbol	Test	Pressure [MPa (psia)]	Peak Power [kW/m(kW/ft)]	Inlet Subcooling [K(°F)]	Initial Temperature [F(°F)]	Elevation [m(in.)]
○	FLECHT SEASET	0.28 (40	1.3 (0.40)	351(140)	1155(1620)	1.83 (72)
●	FLECHT SEASET	0.28 (40)	2.3 (0.70)	342(125)	1144(1600)	1.83 (72)
△	SKEWED	0.28 (40)	2.3 (0.70)	351(140)	1144(1600)	3.05 (120)
□	COSINE	0.28 (40)	3.1 (0.95)	295(40)	1144(1600)	1.83 (72)
■	COSINE	0.28 (40)	3.1 (0.95)	295(40)	1144(1600)	1.98 (78)
◇	COSINE	0.28 (40)	2.4 (0.73)	351(140)	1144(1600)	1.83 (72)
◆	COSINE	0.28 (40)	2.5 (0.75)	351(140)	1144(1600)	1.98 (78)
■	SKEWED	0.14 (20)	2.3 (0.70)	323(90)	1144(1600)	3.05 (120)

6 9423

Figure 2.6 Flooding Rate vs. Temperature Rise

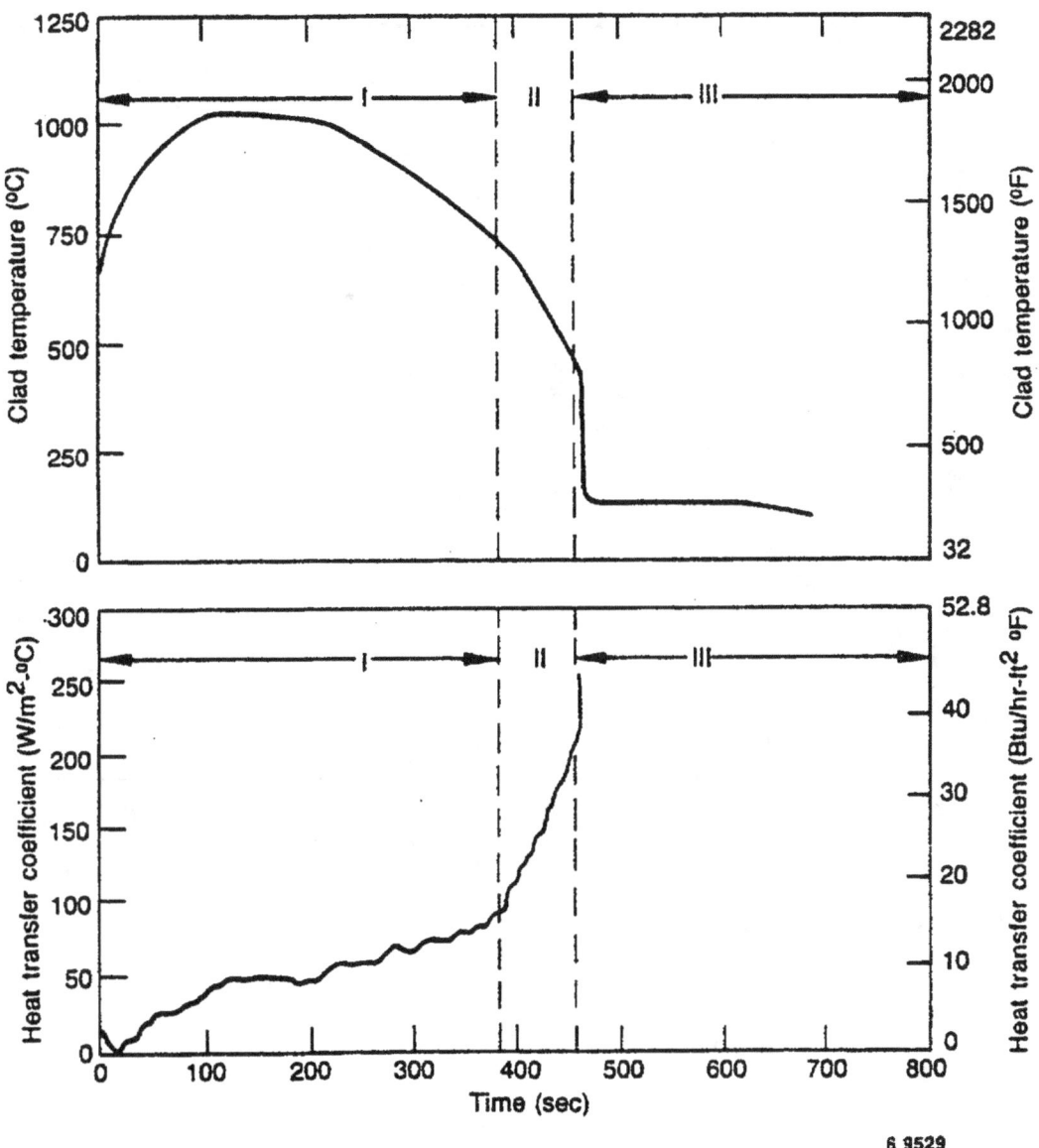

Figure 2.7 Clad Temperature and Heat Transfer
Coefficient in Different Zones

6 9529

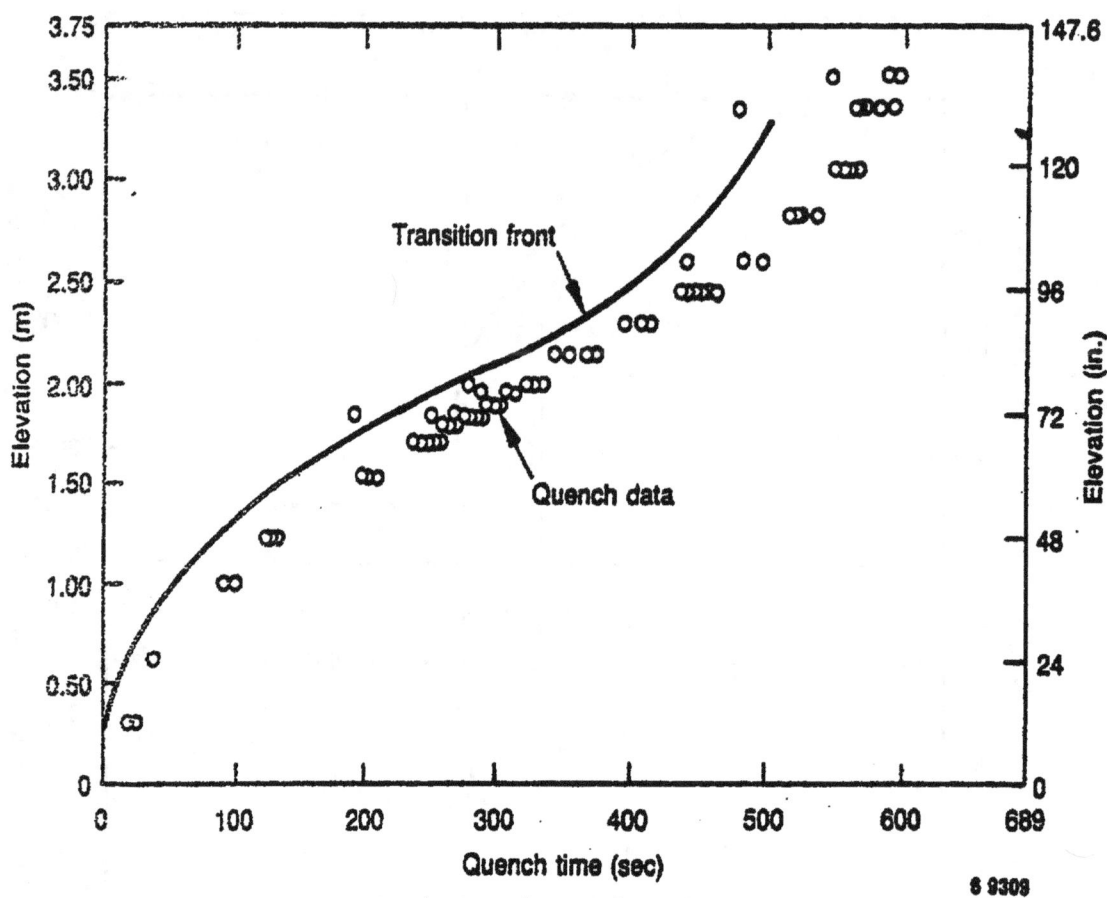

Figure 2.8 Transition Front Relative to Quench Data in Slow Reflood

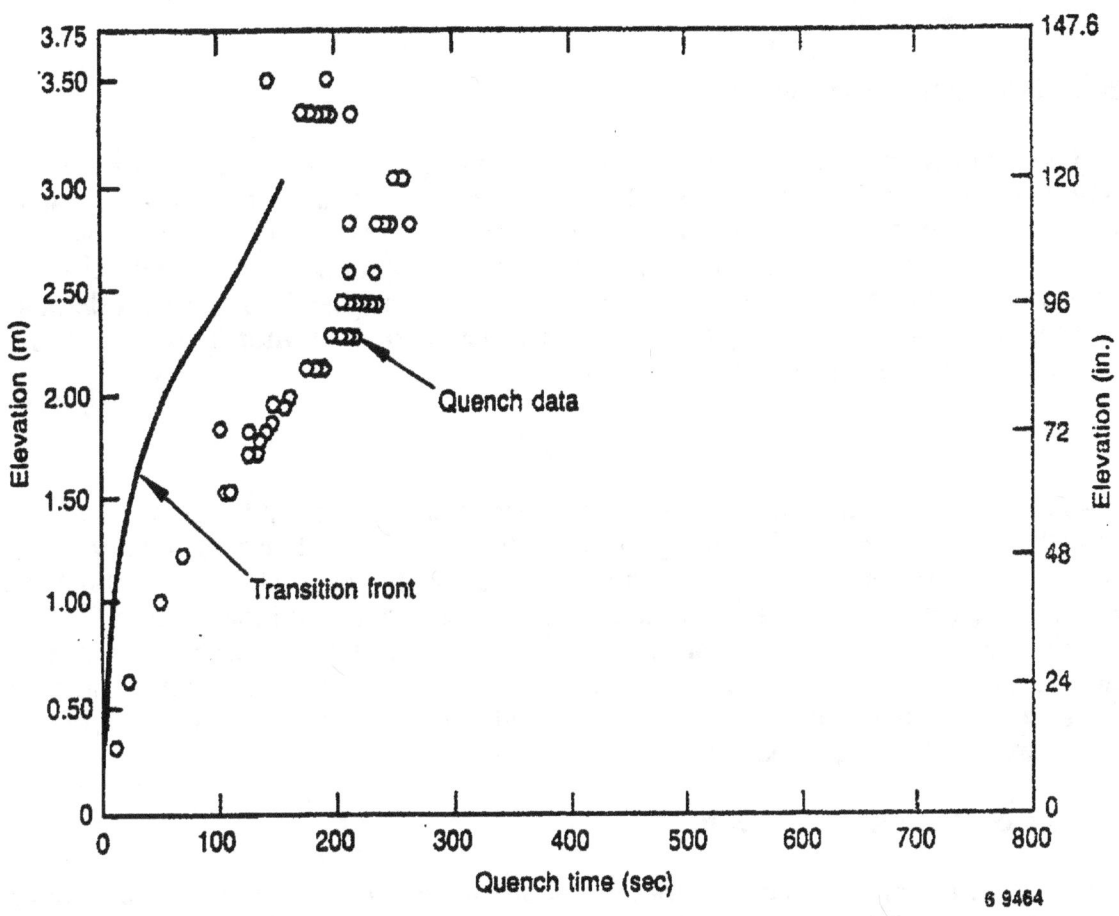

Figure 2.9 Transition Front Relative to Quench Data in Fast
Reflood

6 9464

Quench front propagation during reflood may also be examined from bundle average void fraction data that is reduced from pressure drop measurements. Figure 2.10 shows the void fraction changes for the 0.0254 m/s (1.0 in/s) reflooding case from the Flecht-Seaset tests. It is seen that the void fraction between 0.0 m and 0.6 m elevations rapidly decreases from a value of 1.0 to a value of zero, indicating that the quench front moves up very quickly and a liquid-only region is established at the bottom of the core. At higher elevations, the rate of change in the void fraction is lower than those at low elevations because of the accumulation of steam generated at low elevations.

2.3.2 Liquid Carryout from the Core

The liquid carryout is an important parameter during reflood since the liquid carried out has not been used in quenching the core. Figure 2.11 presents the variation of a time-integrated liquid carryout fraction versus time. The higher the flooding rate, the more rapid the carryout fraction approaches its asymptotic value. This is expected, simply because of the accelerated pace of events occurring at higher flooding rates. The same trend has also been observed in the previous FLECHT tests. The principal effect of increasing flooding rates is to proportionately increase the mass flow above the quench front.

2.3.3 Fuel Assembly

In the Flecht-Seaset program, the bundle geometry was changed from that in the FLECHT program with 15X15 PWR core geometry to reflect the 17X17 PWR core geometry. The program had several subprograms, including some tests with blocked bundles. The 161-rod unblocked bundle tests serve as a reference for comparison with the blocked bundle, as well as for comparison with FLECHT which contained 15X15 core geometry. Comparison of test data indicated that the change from 15X15 to 17X17 bundle geometry did not change the reflood characteristics. Results indicate that uncertainties attributable to other parameters are greater than those introduced by changes in bundle geometry.

2.4 Summary of Code Requirements

The top-level requirement is, no doubt, that the equations in the code represent appropriate physics in order to predict all of these phenomena. An assessment of whether this requirement has been satisfactorily fulfilled is performed by reviewing the code models. If the review indicates that this requirement is satisfactorily fulfilled, the next level of requirements is that trends and important parameters should be predicted with acceptable accuracy. Primary trends are listed below:

(1) The flooding rate has a first order effect on thermal-hydraulic phenomena. Clad temperatures and time of quenching decrease with increasing flooding rates. Flow regimes are dependent upon flooding rates and temperatures. They play an important role in determining cladding temperatures and time of quenching. At the quench front, the stored energy of the rod is released over a short length. Rod temperatures decrease suddenly as the rod quenches.

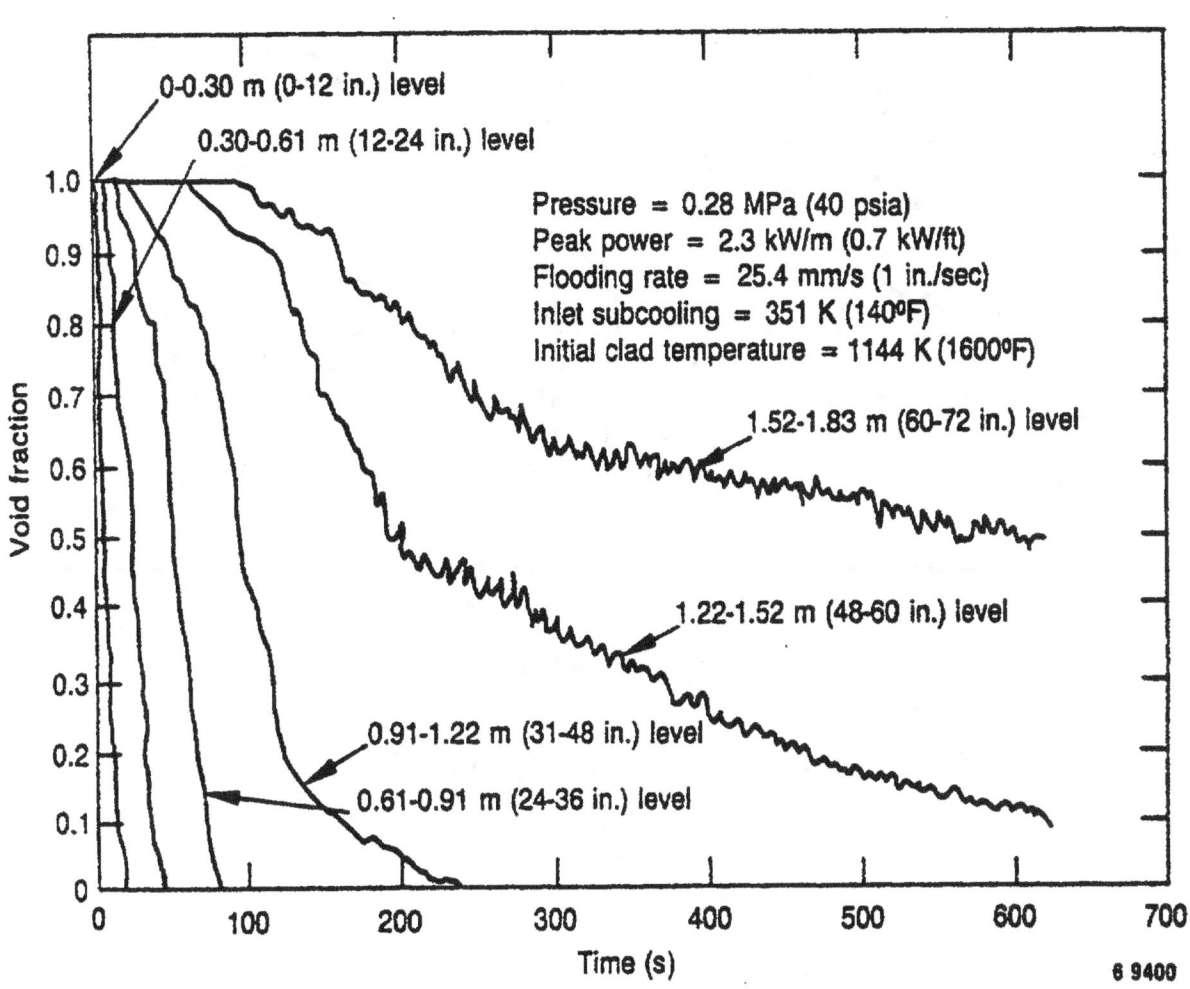

Figure 2.10 Void Fraction Variation with Time During Reflood

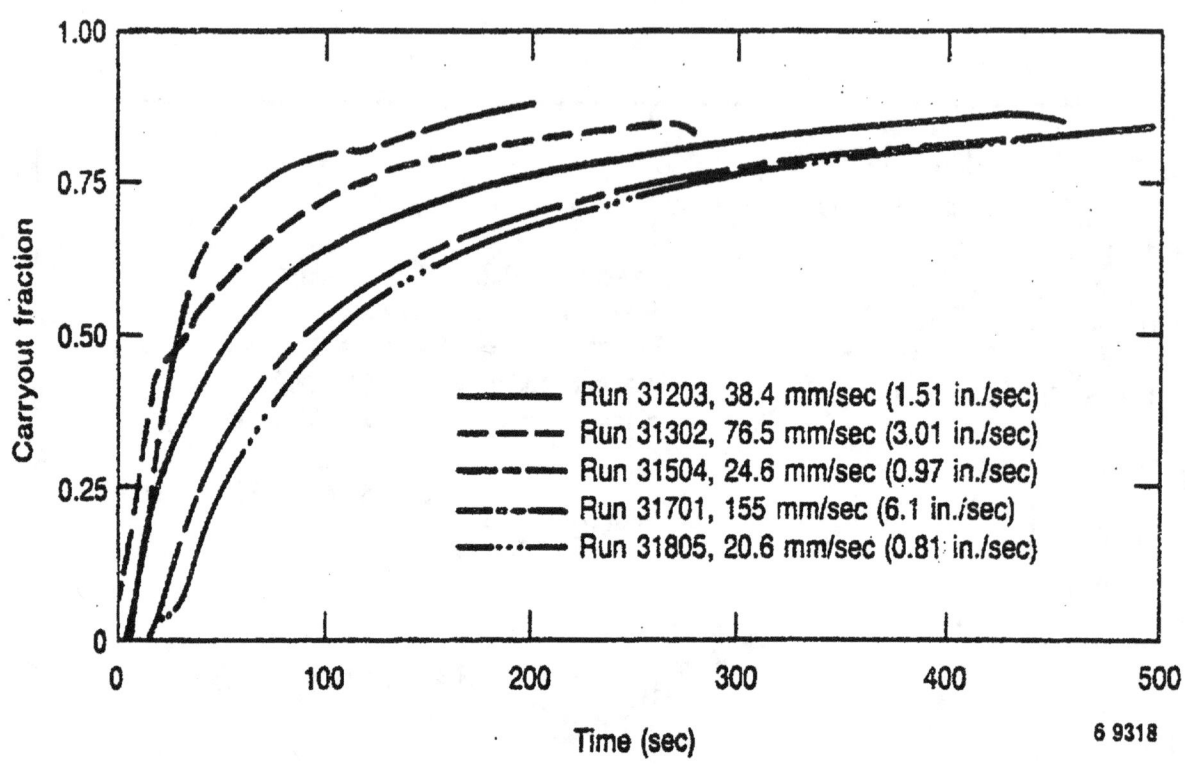

Figure 2.11 Carryout Fraction vs. Time

(2) The flow regimes ahead of the quench front are characterized by a transition or froth region. The length of this transition region is a direct function of the reflooding rate. It is observed that the higher the reflooding rate, the longer is the transition zone. The heat transfer mechanism in the transition zone is different from that in the dispersed flow regime zone and that in the quenching zone.

(3) Bottom reflood progresses very quickly during the onset of reflood; however, intense steam generation soon retards the overall progression of the quench front to a relatively uniform progression. Nevertheless, good core quenching rates are achieved even for flooding rates of 1 inch per second. Some of the liquid is carried out, and is not available to cool the core. The amount of liquid carried out is affected by upper plenum geometry and other system effects.

Important parameters are listed below:

1. clad temperatures

2. vapor fraction and differential pressures at different elevations

3. steam temperatures

4. liquid and steam carryout

Acceptable accuracies can be judged from the spread of experimental data. An example of success metrics for reflood phenomena for Flecht-Seaset Run 31504 is developed in Section 4.

SECTION 3

SYSTEM DESCRIPTION

3.1 Facility Configuration

The Flecht-Seaset test facility was developed by modifying the existing FLECHT test facility. A detailed description of the facility is presented in Ref. 3. Figure 3.1 shows the configuration of the modified facility used to conduct unblocked bundle forced reflood tests. The facility was further modified for gravity reflood tests by adding a downcomer. For steam cooling tests, the facility was again modified to take steam from outside sources.

The facility modifications applicable to all tests are as follows:

(1) a new low-mass housing test section and upper and lower plenums

(2) an upper plenum baffle to improve liquid carryover separation

(3) a 161-rod bundle and related instrumentation

(4) a new pressurized-water supply accumulator and injection line with three rotameters and a turbine meter to measure injection rates from 10 mm/sec (0.4 in/sec) to 150 mm/sec (6.0 in/sec) in forced flooding tests, and up to 6.49 kg/s (14.3 lb/s) in gravity reflood tests

(5) a close-coupled carryover tank connected to the test section upper plenum with a storage capacity of 65.8 kg (145 lb)

(6) a steam separator with a storage capacity of approximately 193 kg (425 lb), a capacity of 0.315 kg/sec (2500 lb/hr), and a liquid collection tank with a volume of 9.5 kg (21 lb) to collect liquid entrained in the exhaust line

(7) exhaust piping with a system pressure control valve and an orifice plate flowmeter to measure exhaust steam flow rates

(8) a commercially available electric steam boiler with a capacity of 0.016 kg/sec (125 lb/hr) of steam production to establish the initial loop pressure and temperature

3.1.1 Forced Reflood Tests and Testing Procedure

The following general procedure was used to establish initial test conditions and perform a typical Flecht-Seaset unblocked bundle reflood test. The accumulator was filled with water and heated to the desired coolant temperature of 53°C (127°F) nominal. The boiler was turned on and brought up to a nominal gage pressure of 0.62 MPa (75 psig). The carryover vessel, steam separator, separator drain tank, test section upper plenum, and test section outlet piping

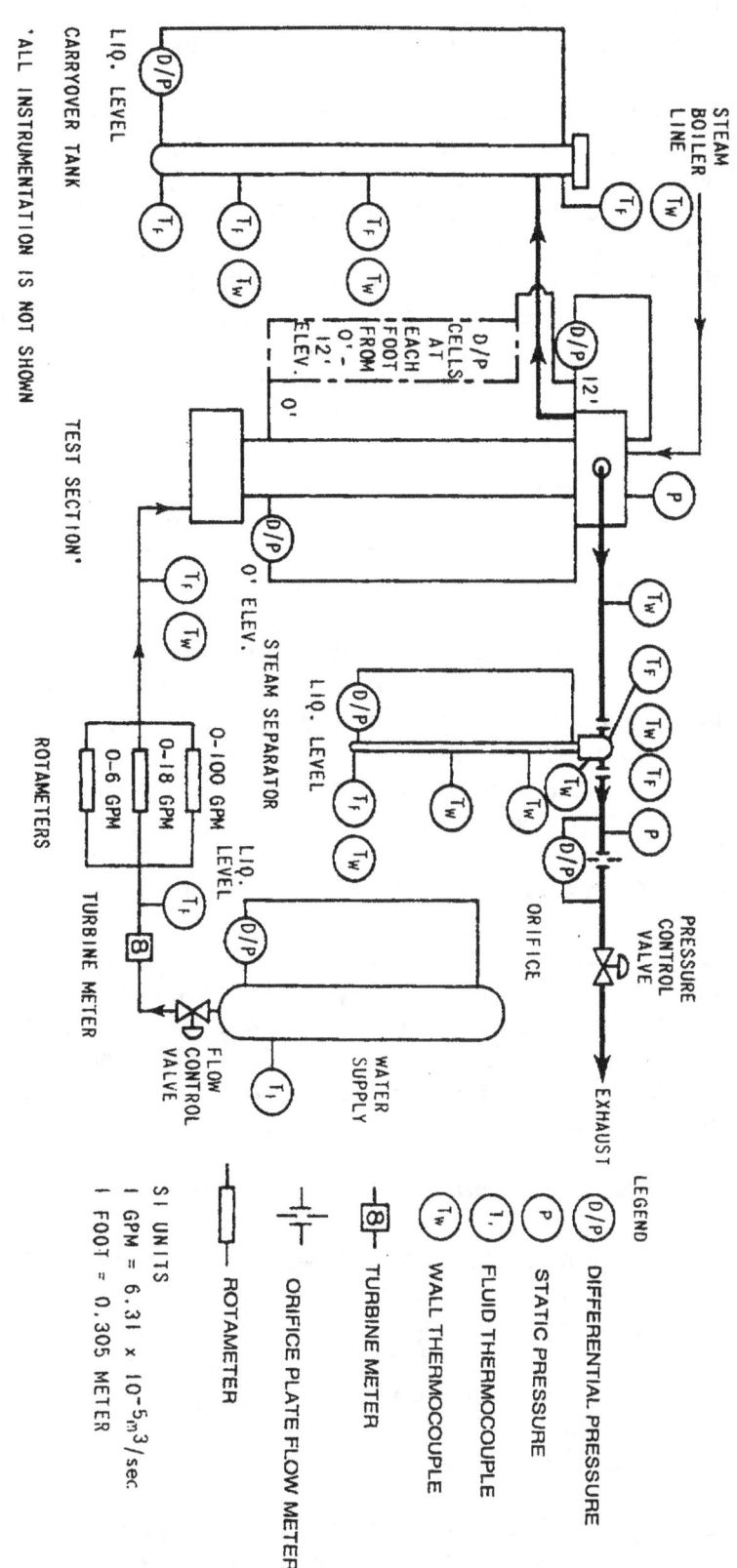

Figure 3.1 Flecht-Seaset System Configuration

(located before the separator) were heated while they were empty to slightly above the saturation temperature corresponding to the test run pressure. The exhaust line between the separator and exhaust orifice was heated to 260°C (500°F) nominal, and the test section lower plenum was heated to the temperature of the coolant in the accumulator. The above component heating was accomplished using clamp-on strip heaters.

The test section, carryover vessel, and exhaust line components were pressurized to the desired system pressure of 0.14 to 0.41 MPa (20 to 60 psia) by valving the steam boiler into the system, and setting the exhaust line control valve to the desired pressure. The coolant in the accumulator was pressurized to 2.76 MPa (400 psia). Water was then injected into the test section lower plenum until it reached the beginning of the heated length of the bundle heater rods. Coolant was circulated and drained to ensure that the water in the lower plenum and injection line were at the specified temperature before the run. Power was then applied to the test bundle and the rods were allowed to heat up. When the temperature in any two designated bundle thermocouples reached a preset value between 260°C and 871°C (500°F to 1600°F), the computer automatically initiated flooding and controlled power decay. Solenoid valves (not shown in Figure 3.1) and a hydraulic control valve controlled the coolant injection into the test section. During a run, the boiler was valved out of the system, and the pressure was maintained at the desired level by the control valve located in the exhaust line. Liquid effluent leaving the test section was separated in the upper plenum and collected in a carryover tank. A baffle assembly in the upper plenum was used to improve liquid carryout separation and minimize liquid entrainment into the exhaust vapor. The separator located in the exhaust line was used to separate any remaining entrained liquid carryout from the vapor. Dry steam flow leaving the separator was measured by an orifice meter before exhausting to the atmosphere. In order to ensure that a single-phase flow measurement was made, the piping upstream of the orifice was heated to a temperature well above the saturation. After all designated heater rods were quenched, as indicated by the rod thermocouples, power to the heater rods and coolant injection to the test section were terminated. The entire system was depressurized by opening the exhaust control valve, and the Computer Data Acquisition System (CDAS) was deactivated. Water stored in all components was drained and weighed.

After runs 30223 through 30817 had been conducted, it was noticed that some water entered the bundle steam probe lines. In order to prevent this occurrence in further tests, a modification was made to the above test procedure. This modification consisted of power pulsing the bundle to approximately 260°C (500°F) before applying the full power. Power pulsing vented the bundle steam probe lines before starting a new run. This procedure was used to dry out the bundle thimbles and steam probes.

3.1.2 Gravity Reflood Tests and Testing Procedure

During the test series, further modifications were made to the facility to conduct gravity reflood tests. Some of the modifications were made to simulate reactor system loop behavior. These modifications consisted of connecting a downcomer to the lower plenum, moving the injection line from the lower plenum to the bottom of the downcomer, installing a resistance orifice plate between the test section outlet pipe and the inlet flange of the entrainment separator to simulate the hot leg resistance, venting the top of the downcomer to the entrainment separator, and installing additional differential pressure cells.

The procedure used to perform the forced reflood tests was also used to perform the gravity reflood tests, with one exception. Specifically, after flooding was initiated, the rate was adjusted, if necessary, to ensure that the level in the downcomer did not go above the 4.88-m (192-in) elevation.

3.1.3 Steam Cooling Tests and Testing Procedure

To obtain steam flow heat transfer data in the rod bundle geometry, a series of low-temperature steam cooling tests was conducted. For these tests, the facility was modified by connecting the lower plenum of the test section to the Flecht-Seaset steam generator facility boiler with a steam line.

The steam cooling tests were initiated by injecting steam at a high flow rate [approximately 0.3 kg/sec (0.6 lb/sec)] into the bundle. When the system reached the saturation condition, the steam flow rate was adjusted to the specified value. When the steam flow was stabilized, a constant bundle power was applied, and the CDAS was activated. The test was terminated when a steady-state condition was achieved. Both transient and steady-state data were recorded.

3.2 Heater Rod Bundle

A cross-section of the test bundle is shown in Figure 3.2 with the heater rod instrumentation groups. The bundle comprised 161 heater rods (93 uninstrumented and 68 instrumented), 4 instrumented thimbles, 12 steam probes, 8 solid triangular fillers, and 8 grids. The triangular fillers were welded to the grids to maintain the proper grid location. The fillers also reduced the amount of excess flow area from 9.3 to 4.7 percent. Locations of electrically heated rods, thimbles, and steam probe tubes are identified by alphanumeric coordinates indicated in Figure 3.2.

Each heater rod is identified by a circle. Some heater rods are instrumented by thermocouples welded inside the cladding. If a rod is instrumented, it is identified by a group number (shown in the circle), which identifies the locations of various thermocouples inside the rod. A cross-section of a heater rod with thermocouple locations is shown in Figure 3.3. The heater rods were designed to provide an axial cosine-shaped power profile. As a run started, the computer provided decay power to the rods. Figures 3.4 and 3.5 show the axial power shape and variation of decay power with time, respectively.

Steam probe tubes and thimbles are identified by double circles in Figure 3.2. Steam probe tubes contain steam probes for measurement of superheated steam temperatures. Steam probes were located in the bundle and in the test section outlet pipe. The bundle steam probes were located in the thimble tubes (Figure 3.6). The probe was designed to separate moisture from the high-temperature steam, and aspirate the steam across the thermocouple and into an ice bucket. Because of a large number of probes, the probes were controlled to limit the amount of steam aspirated from the test section. This was accomplished by manifolding the aspiration lines for common elevations of steam probes together, and closing the lines when the particular elevation had quenched.

The probe in the outlet pipe was installed in the elbow of the test section outlet pipe. This probe, which measured the temperature of the steam leaving the test section, was designed to measure steam temperature in the same manner as the bundle probes. The end of the thermocouple was formed so that it did not touch the walls of the 6.4-mm (0.25-in.) diameter tubing. Thermocouples were welded to the inside of thimble walls to measure their temperature.

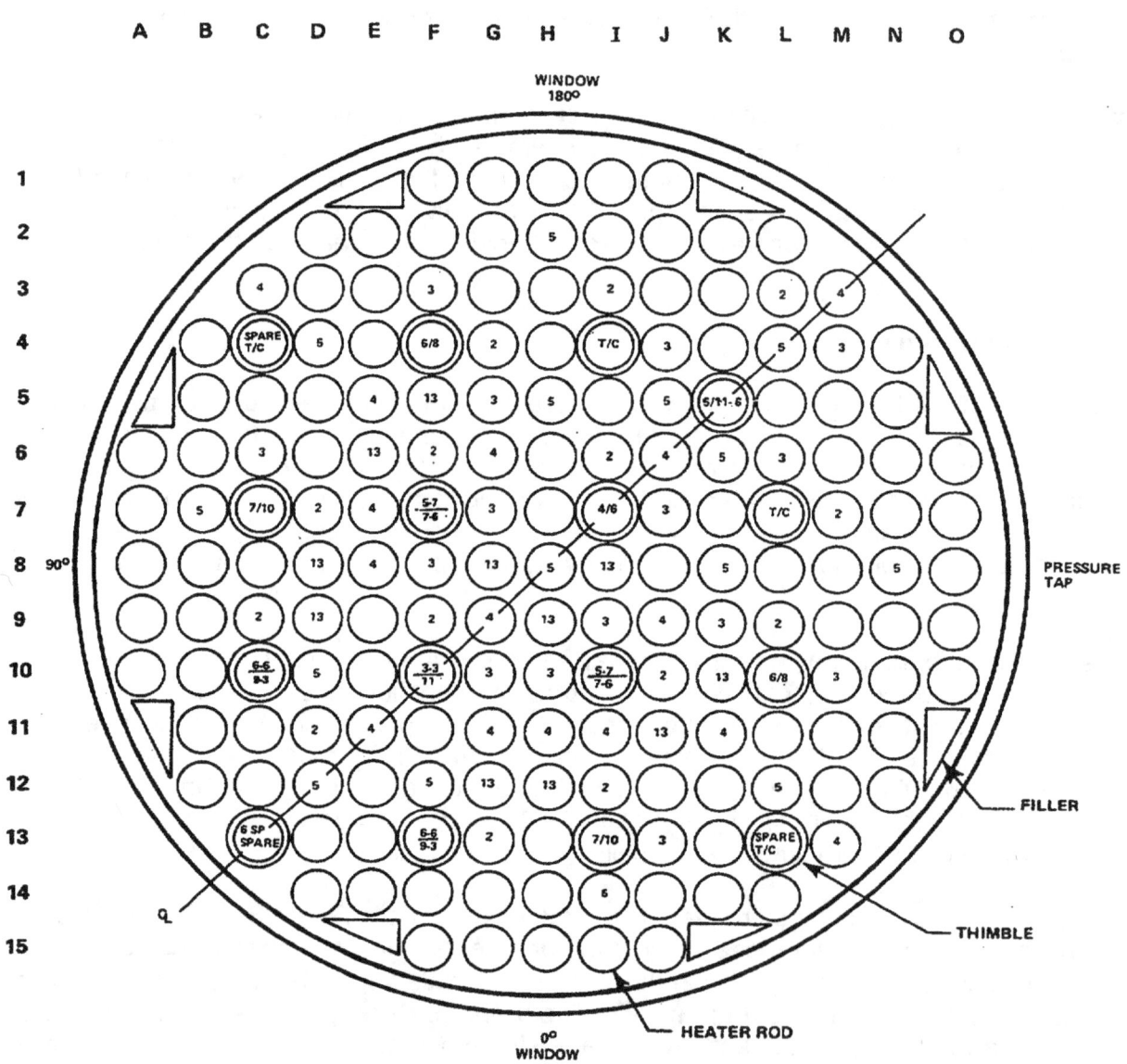

Figure 3.2   Flecht-Seaset 161-Rod Test Bundle

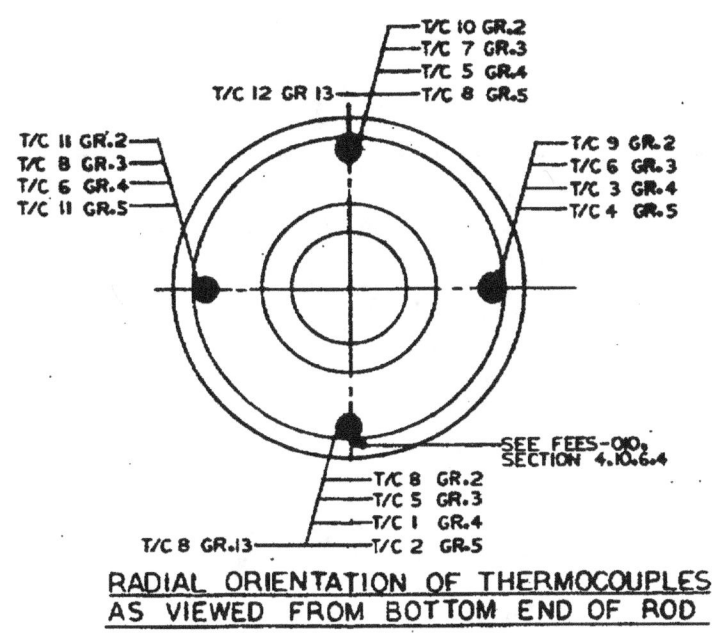

RADIAL ORIENTATION OF THERMOCOUPLES
AS VIEWED FROM BOTTOM END OF ROD

Figure 3.3   Heater Rod Thermocouple
Locations

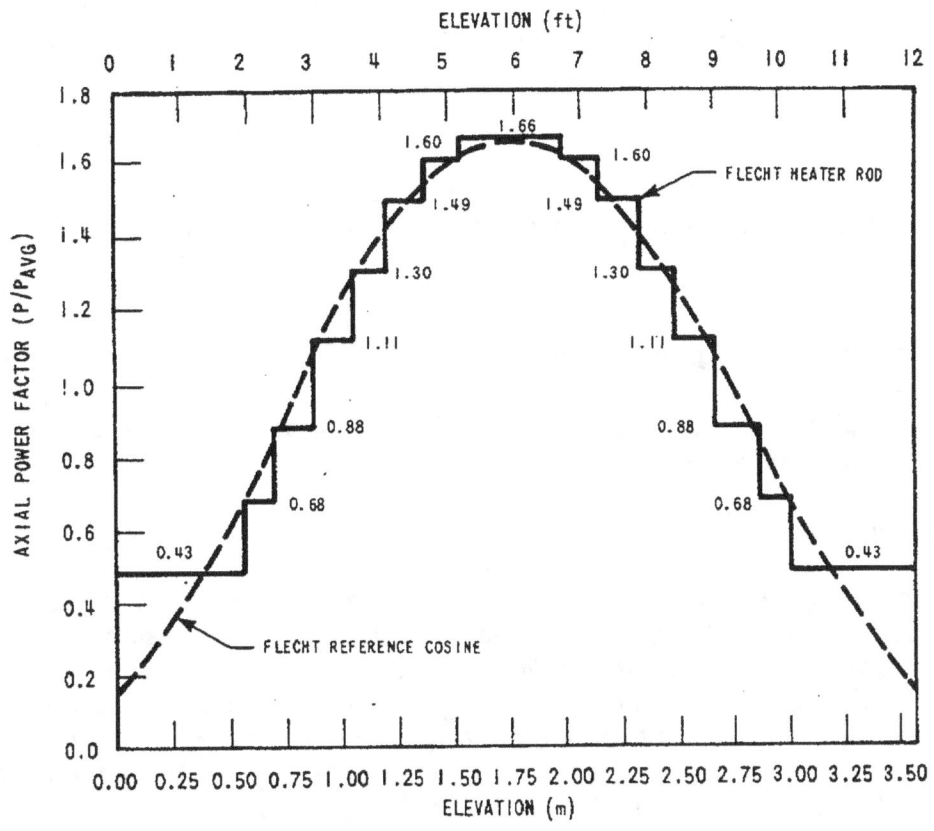

Figure 3.4 Flecht-Seaset Axial Power Shape

-28-

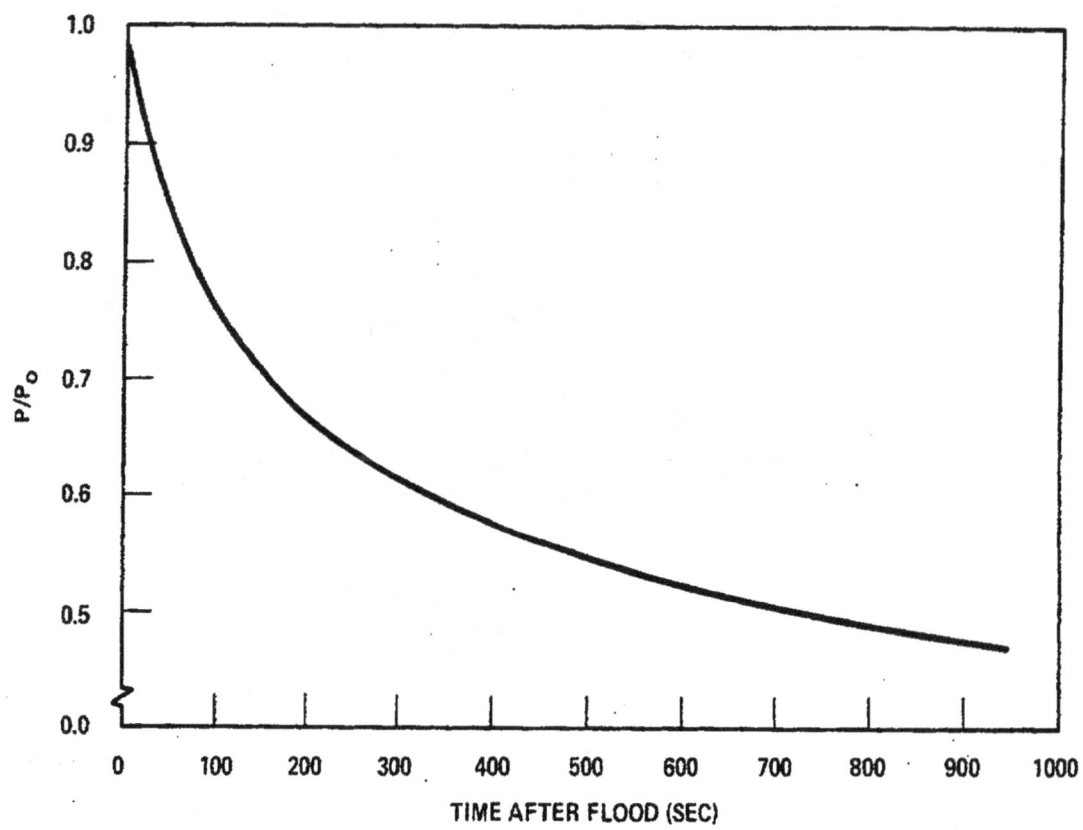

Figure 3.5 Decay Power Curve (ANS + 20%)

3.3 Discussion of System Design Features

The following paragraphs describe the major design features that were used for the Flecht-Seaset unblocked bundle test series.

3.3.1 Low-Mass Housing

A low-mass housing design was used in the previous FLECHT test series to minimize the housing effects. The effect of the housing on heater rod temperatures was studied by performing two tests with the same initial conditions except for the housing wall initial temperatures. The effect of the cold and hot housing on the rod surface temperature and the corresponding heat transfer coefficient, *excluding the peripheral rods*, was found to be negligible. In addition, the hot and cold housing did not affect the quench front along the bundle. It was concluded that performing reflood tests with an unheated low-mass housing was acceptable, since a cold housing did not significantly affect the reflood heat transfer and hydraulic behavior of the rod bundle.

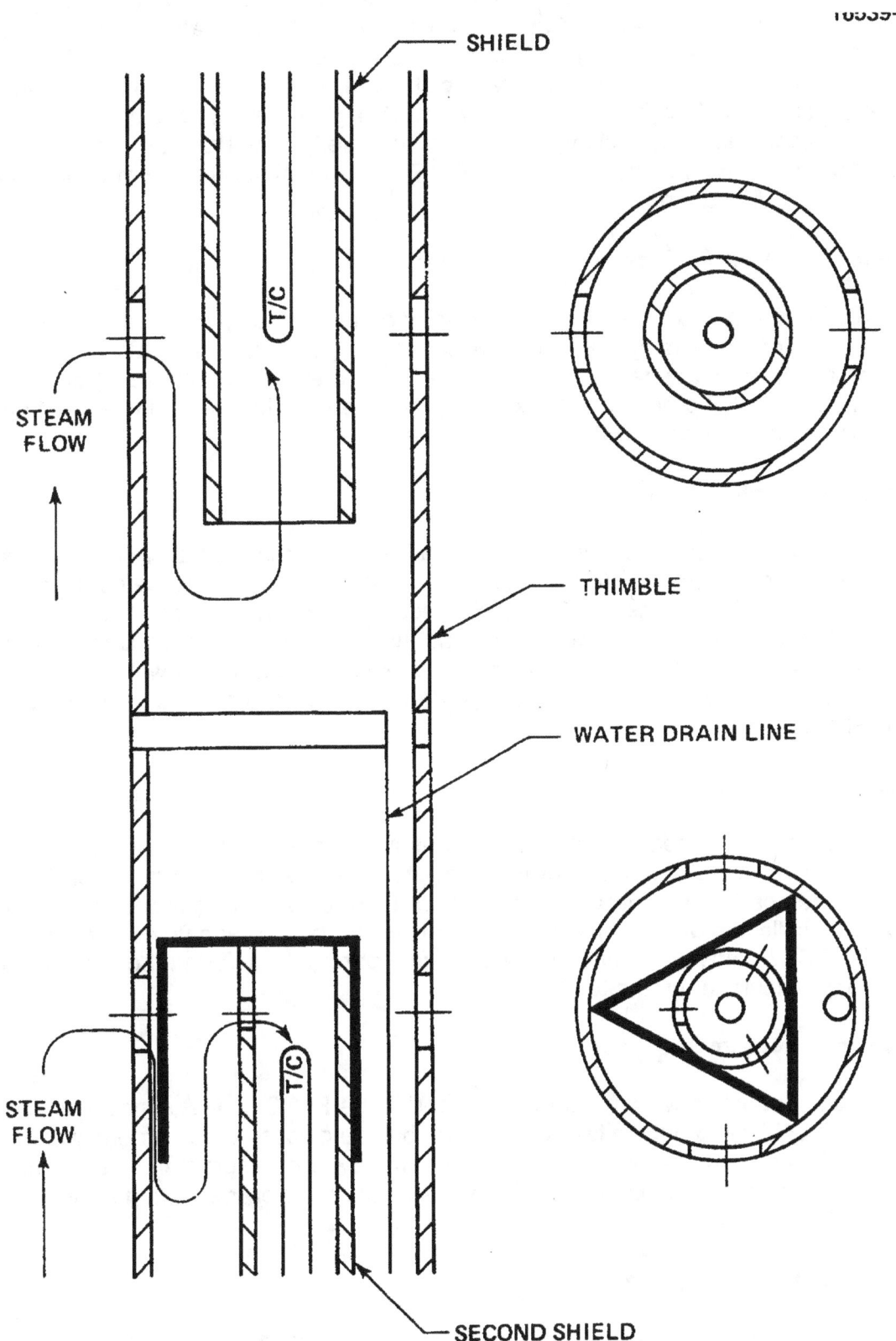

SHIELD

T/C

STEAM
FLOW

STEAM
FLOW

THIMBLE

WATER DRAIN LINE

T/C

SECOND SHIELD

Figure D-6. Steam Probe Design

Figure 3.6 Steam Probe Design

The housing was constructed of 304 stainless steel, and is rated for 0.52 MPa (60 psig) at 816°C (1500°F). The design allowed for 1,000 pressure and temperature cycles. Two quartz sight glasses were located 180 degrees apart at the 0.91-, 1.83-, and 2.74-m (36-, 72-, and 108-in) elevations for viewing and photographic study in some selected runs. The sight glass configuration allowed backlighting as well as frontlighting for the purpose of photographic studies. The sight glasses had clamp-on heaters to raise the quartz temperature at the initiation of reflood to approximately 260°C (500°F). This eliminated the formation of a liquid film on the quartz during a run.

3.3.2 Bundle Differential Pressure Cells

The test section differential pressure cells provided data used to calculate a mass balance and bundle void fraction. Low-range [+ 0.0069 MPa (+ 1 psi)] pressure transducers were used to improve the accuracy of the data. The cells were located every 0.30 m (12 in) along the test section. The differential pressure cell manifold was carefully bled to eliminate any trapped air and, thus, improve the repeatability of the readings.

3.3.3 Pressure Control

Maintaining a constant upper plenum pressure had been a difficult problem in previous FLECHT test programs. In an effort to reduce the pressure oscillations, several modifications were made to the facility for the FLECHT test series. The first modification was to increase the volume of the steam separator to help reduce the magnitude of the oscillations. The second modification was to replace the air-operated globe exhaust control valve with an air operated V-ball control valve. The V-ball valve had a larger flow loss coefficient, and a more linear operating characteristic.

3.3.4 Facility Operation

The test facility was designed for automatic operation whenever critical functions required a high degree of sophistication, safety, or repeatability. The Computer Data Acquisition System (CDAS) was the heart of the operation. It monitored, protected, and controlled the facility operation, and collected data. It also controlled pressure, power, and flow during the test. In addition, the CDAS software monitored critical safety parameters during the test, and used corresponding outputs to run the test.

3.3.5 Power Measurement

The technique of bundle power measurement used in the FLECHT test series was used again for the present unblocked bundle test series. The bundle power measurement systems were improved by the addition of a secondary independent power measurement system, and the adoption of a system calibration. Details of the secondary power measuring system are presented in Ref. 3.

3.3.6 Coolant Injection System

The facility configuration (Figure 3.1) shows the coolant injection system, which consisted of a hydraulic valve for programmed flow and a turbine meter in series with three rotameters. The flow out of the rotameters went either to the lower plenum of the test section for forced reflood, or to the bottom elbow of the downcomer for gravity reflood. Solenoid valves were used to initiate flooding and to channel the flow through the desired rotameter. A bidirectional turbo-probe in the downcomer crossover pipe measured the flow between the downcomer and the test section in the gravity reflood tests. In the steam cooling configuration, the steam was supplied to the lower plenum from the boiler. The steam flow rate was measured by a vortex meter used on the steam generator facility.

3.3.7 Data Acquisition Systems

Data acquisition was accomplished by the following systems.

Computer Data Acquisition System (CDAS)

The CDAS, the primary data collecting system used on the Flecht-Seaset unblocked bundle facility, consisted of a PDP-11 computer and associated equipment. The system could record 256 channels of analog input data representing bundle and system and fluid temperatures, displaying temperature directly in degrees Fahrenheit. A Fluke recorder also recorded millivolt data from the test section differential pressure cells, allowing the operator to monitor the operation and repeatability of the differential pressure cells.

Multiple-Pen Strip Chart Recorders

Six Texas Instruments strip chart recorders were used to record 1) bundle power; 2) selected bundle thermocouple readings; 3) reflood line rotameter and turbine meter flows; 4) turbo probe flows; 5) accumulator, separator drain tank, housing, and carryover tank levels; 6) exhaust orifice differential pressure; and 7) selected bundle steam probe thermocouple readings. These recorders gave the loop operators and test directors immediate information on the test progress and warning in the event of any system anomalies.

3.4 Instrumentation

The instrumentation on the unblocked bundle facility was designed to measure temperature, pressure, flow, liquid level, and power. The temperature data were recorded by type K (chromel-alumel) thermocouples using 66°C (150°F) reference junctions. The liquid level and pressure data, both static and differential, were measured by balanced bridge strain gage transducers. Power input to the bundle was measured by Hall-effect watt transducers, which produce a direct current electrical output proportional to the power input. The fluid flow measurements were made by a turbine meter and rotameters for coolant injection, an orifice with a differential pressure transducer for exhaust steam flow, and a bidirectional turbo-probe for downcomer crossover flow during gravity reflood.

3.4.1 Heater Rod Bundle Instrumentation

The bundle instrumentation is described in Section 3.2. Not all of the available instrumentation in the bundle was recorded because of the 256-channel limit of the CDAS. However, 205 thermocouples, including those pertaining to heater rods, thimbles, and steam probes, were recorded by the CDAS.

3.4.2 Test Section Instrumentation

The upper and lower plenums had fluid thermocouples. The upper plenum had a differential pressure transducer to measure liquid collection rates, a static pressure transducer to measure the test section pressure, and a static pressure transducer (not recorded) to provide a control signal to the V-ball exhaust valve. The low-mass housing had differential pressure transducers located every 0.30 m (12 in.) along the heated length of the bundle and one differential pressure transducer to obtain a liquid level and average bundle void fraction over the entire heated length.

3.4.3 Carryover Tank Instrumentation

The carryover tank was instrumented with two wall thermocouples and one fluid thermocouple. A differential pressure transducer was used to measure the liquid collected in the tank as a function of time.

3.4.4 Steam Separator Instrumentation

The steam separator was instrumented with three wall thermocouples and a differential pressure transducer for measuring the entrained liquid carryout rate. The steam separator drain tank was instrumented with two wall thermocouples, one fluid thermocouple, and a differential pressure transducer for measuring the entrained liquid carryout rate.

3.4.5 Exhaust Pipe Instrumentation

The exhaust pipe was equipped with a differential pressure transducer connected across an orifice plate for measuring single-phase steam flow. A fluid thermocouple and a static pressure transducer were used to determine exhaust steam thermodynamic conditions. Two wall thermocouples were used to record exhaust line temperatures during heat-up and the experimental run. A steam probe located in the exhaust line measured the temperature of the steam leaving the upper plenum.

3.4.6 Accumulator Tank Instrumentation

Accumulator tank instrumentation included a fluid thermocouple and a differential pressure transducer for measurement of liquid level.

3.4.7 Injection Line Instrumentation

Injection line instrumentation consisted of a 3.78×10^{-5} to 3.78×10^{-3} m^3 /sec (0.6 to 60 gal/min) turbine meter to measure coolant injection with three rotameters, 0 to 3.78×10^{-4}, 0 to 1.14×10^{-3}, and 0 to 6.31×10^{-3} m^3 /sec (0 to 6, 0 to 18, and 0 to 100 gal/min), as a redundant measurement. Two fluid thermocouples were used to measure coolant injection temperatures.

SECTION 4

TRAC-M ASSESSMENT
WITH
FLECHT-SEASET REFLOOD TEST DATA, RUN 31504

4.1 Success Metrics

Validation of thermal-hydraulic codes requires comparison of code predictions to experimental data. The success metrics are used to judge how well the code is validated. There are qualitative and quantitative metrics. The recently completed RELAP5 adequacy assessment effort presents important concepts that define these criteria. Part of these concepts is repeated here for convenience. Additional concepts on providing "User Guidelines" are added here.

(1) "Excellent agreement" applies when the code exhibits no deficiencies in modeling a given behavior. Major and minor phenomena and trends are correctly predicted. The calculated results are judged to agree closely with the data. With few exceptions, the calculations will lie within the specified or inferred uncertainty bands of the data. The code may be used with confidence in similar applications. The term "major phenomena" refers to phenomena that influence key parameters, such as rod cladding temperature, pressure, differential pressure, mass flow rate, and mass distribution. Predicting the major trends means that the prediction shows the significant features of the data. Significant features include the magnitude of a given parameter through the transient, slopes, and inflection points that mark significant changes in the parameter.

(2) "Reasonable agreement" applies when the code exhibits minor deficiencies. Overall, the code provides an acceptable prediction. All major trends and phenomena are correctly predicted. Differences between calculated values and data are greater than those that are deemed necessary for "excellent agreement." The calculation frequently lies outside but near the specified or inferred uncertainty bands of the data. However, the correct conclusions about trends and phenomena would be reached if the code were used in similar applications. The code models and/or facility model noding should be reviewed to see if improvements can be made.

(3) "Minimal agreement" applies when the code exhibits significant deficiencies. Overall, the code provides a prediction that is not acceptable. Some major trends or phenomena are not correctly predicted, and some calculated values lie considerably outside the specified or inferred uncertainty bands of the data. Incorrect conclusions about trends and phenomena may be reached if the code were used in similar applications. If the agreement is "Minimal," the model noding must be reviewed, and sensitivity studies using different noding or options should be performed. The selection of nodalizations or options should not be arbitrary, and it should be aimed to model the phenomena more accurately. If the agreement can be improved with different noding or options, it can be reclassified as "Reasonable" or "Excellent." In this case, new "User Guidelines" should be developed. If the agreement cannot be improved, it should be reclassified as "Insufficient agreement," as described below.

(4) "Insufficient agreement" applies when the code exhibits major deficiencies, and provides an unacceptable prediction of the test data because major trends are not correctly predicted. Most calculated values lie outside the specified or inferred uncertainty bands of the data, and incorrect conclusions about trends and phenomena are almost certain if the code is used in similar applications. An appropriate warning must be issued to users. Selected code models should be reviewed and modified and, if necessary, new models should be developed and assessed before the code can be used with confidence in similar applications.

Quantitative metrics define requirements for accuracy of code predictions of the test data. The accuracy depends on two elements. The first is the "goodness" of code models. Accuracy of the predictions depends on how realistically code models simulate phenomena. The second is the experimental data spread. Discussions below show how the goodness of the code models and test data characteristics affect the accuracy of predictions.

The assessment of the TRAC-P code, an earlier version of the TRAC-M code, concluded that the modeling of physics of the grid spacers was inadequate. Therefore, the option to include grid spacer models should not be used (Ref. 15). Analysis of the reflood phenomena in Section 2 indicates that grid spacers substantially contribute to cooling of the rod cladding. Any calculation without the grid spacer effect should indicate hotter cladding temperatures for the rods. TRAC-M calculations will be biased because of the absence of grid spacer effects. The best way to quantify this bias is to compare experimental data of cladding temperatures with and without grid spacers. The effect of grid spacers on heat transfer has been studied for reflood conditions in the Flooding Experiments with Blocked Arrays (FEBA) test series, which shows that the effect of grid spacers on cladding temperatures is approximately 100 K. Hence, we should expect approximately 100 K of bias in code predictions.

The next important element in determining a quantitative metric is the experimental data spread, which differs from the instrument uncertainty that addresses the accuracy in measuring with an instrument. The experimental data spread (the uncertainty band of the test data) occurs because of the random nature of the phenomena. In the Flecht-Seaset reflood experiments, the reflood is considered to be one dimensional since the geometry of the test section and the rod bundle is one-dimensional. Hence, the input deck is built on the basis of one-dimensional assumptions. The code will calculate one cladding temperature at a specific location of the rod at each time step of the calculation. The rod modeled in the input deck represents all similar rods. However, in reality, the two-phase flow in the test section has some randomness in that all water slugs are not of the same length or shape, all droplets are not of the same size or shape, and their concentrations vary from location to location within the test section. Hence, one should neither expect that maximum cladding temperatures occur in all rods at the same time in the same horizontal plane although the power shape for each rod is the same, nor expect that all rods quench at the same time in the same horizontal plane. There will be a normal spread of experimental data attributable to the random nature of the two-phase flow. The code will predict only one average value for the maximum rod surface temperature. For an "Excellent" agreement, the prediction can be at the edge of the spread of the maximum rod surface temperature data. This spread will form part of the quantitative metric.

Figures 4.1 through 4.4 show clad temperatures measured at different elevations and at different rods. The lowest spread occurs at lower levels, and the spread increases with increasing elevation. At higher elevations, droplets move randomly in many directions, and their sizes and shapes vary. Clad temperatures at a horizontal plane can vary as much as 100 K. Thermocouples are located at different rods in a horizontal plane. These give multiple measurements at a given elevation. These measurements not only show that a spread of 100 K can occur in clad temperatures; they also indicate that quenching times at high elevations may vary up to 120 s. Thermocouples affected by the housing wall and those giving clearly erroneous readings are not included in these plots.

However, similar multiple measurements are not available for other parameters such as pressure drops. For pressure drop measurements, there is only one pair of pressure taps available to measure each pressure drop between two elevations. Hence, for pressure drops it is not possible to determine the data spread or uncertainty bands caused by randomness of two-phase flow. Similarly, steam probe measurements are made at few unpowered rods at selected elevations. It is assumed that these measured quantities give the average quantities for a horizontal plane. Hence, assessment of these parameters can only be made qualitatively.

In summary, a quantitative metric for clad temperature predictions is a bias of 100 K and a spread of 100 K. This would make a total of 200 K difference in predictions. The quenching time spread is 120 s. The assessment of the remaining parameters will be made qualitatively.

4.2 TRAC Input Model for Flecht-Seaset Forced Reflood Run 31504

Figure 4.5 shows the TRAC input model schematic used to model forced flow reflood in Flecht-Seaset Run 31504. The input deck contains a single one-dimensional vessel component (Component 5) modeling the test section and plenums, one fill component (Component 1) where the flow rate is defined, a break component (Component 4) where the system pressure is defined, and two pipe components (Components 3 and 2) connecting the break and fill components, respectively. The fuel (heater) rods are modeled using a rod component (Component 6), and the test section housing wall is modeled using another rod component (Component 7).

A one-dimensional vessel component is used since the reflood phenomenon that occurs in the Flecht-Seaset test section is one-dimensional. That component contains 18 cells, the lower plenum is modeled with cells 1 and 2, the rod bundle occupies cells 3 through 17, and the upper plenum is modeled with cell 18. The 161 heater rods are modeled as a single rod component. The input deck does not model grid spacers since the effects of grid spacers on thermal-hydraulic phenomena are not correctly modeled in the TRAC code (Ref. 15). Coolant injection was applied to the lower plenum through the pipe and fill components, and the flow exits from the break component.

The axial power shape modeling using 18 axial cells accurately duplicated the axial power shape as constructed in heater rods including all steps indicating different power levels. This was done in order to accurately compare predictions of temperatures with measured values. This is much finer nodalization than that used for standard reactor fuel rod modeling. Normally, fuel rods are modeled using three or four axial elevations. When a coarse nodalization is used, there will be an additional uncertainty in calculations that should be accounted for.

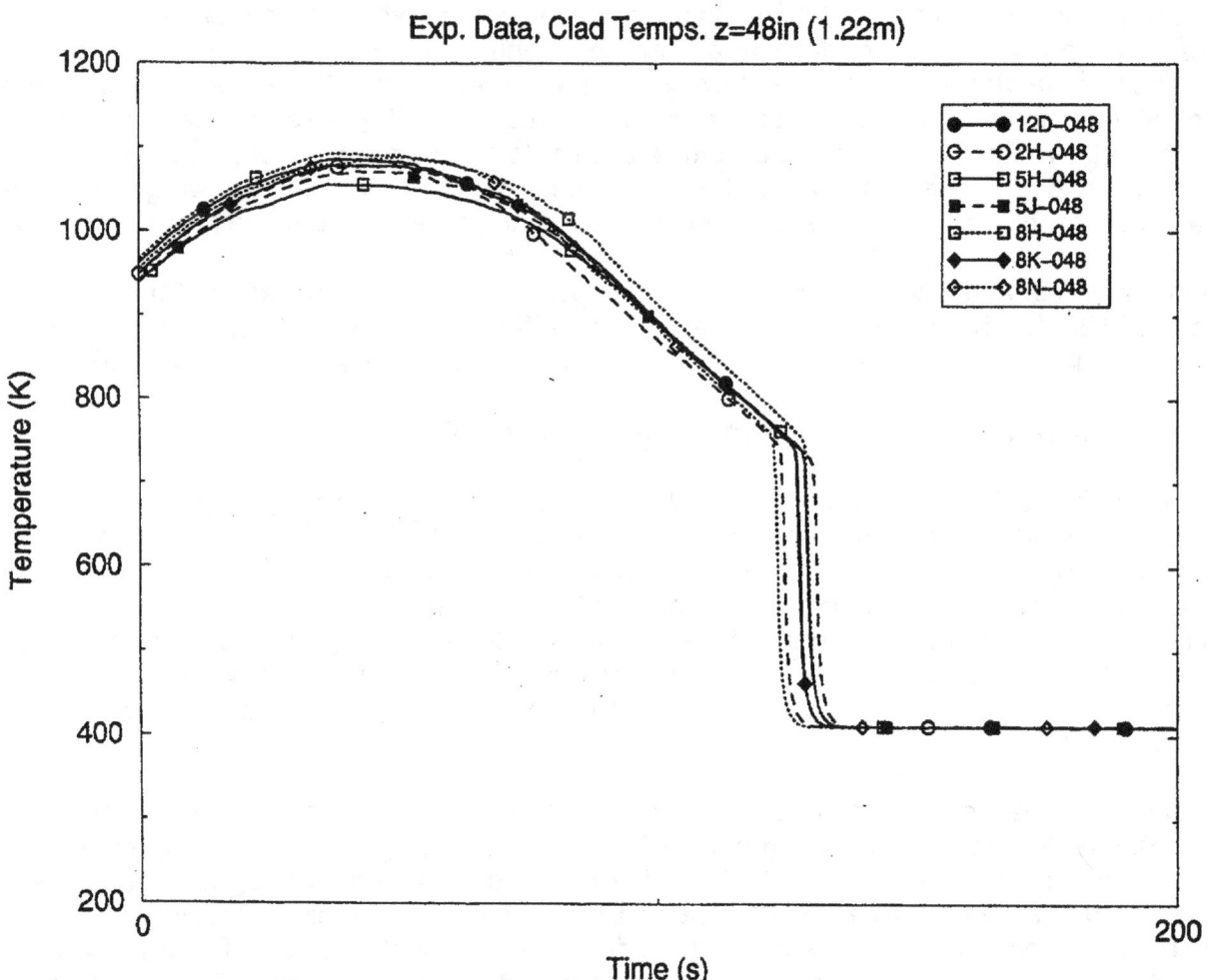

Figure 4.1 Flecht-Seaset 31504 Exp. Clad Temperatures, z=1.22m

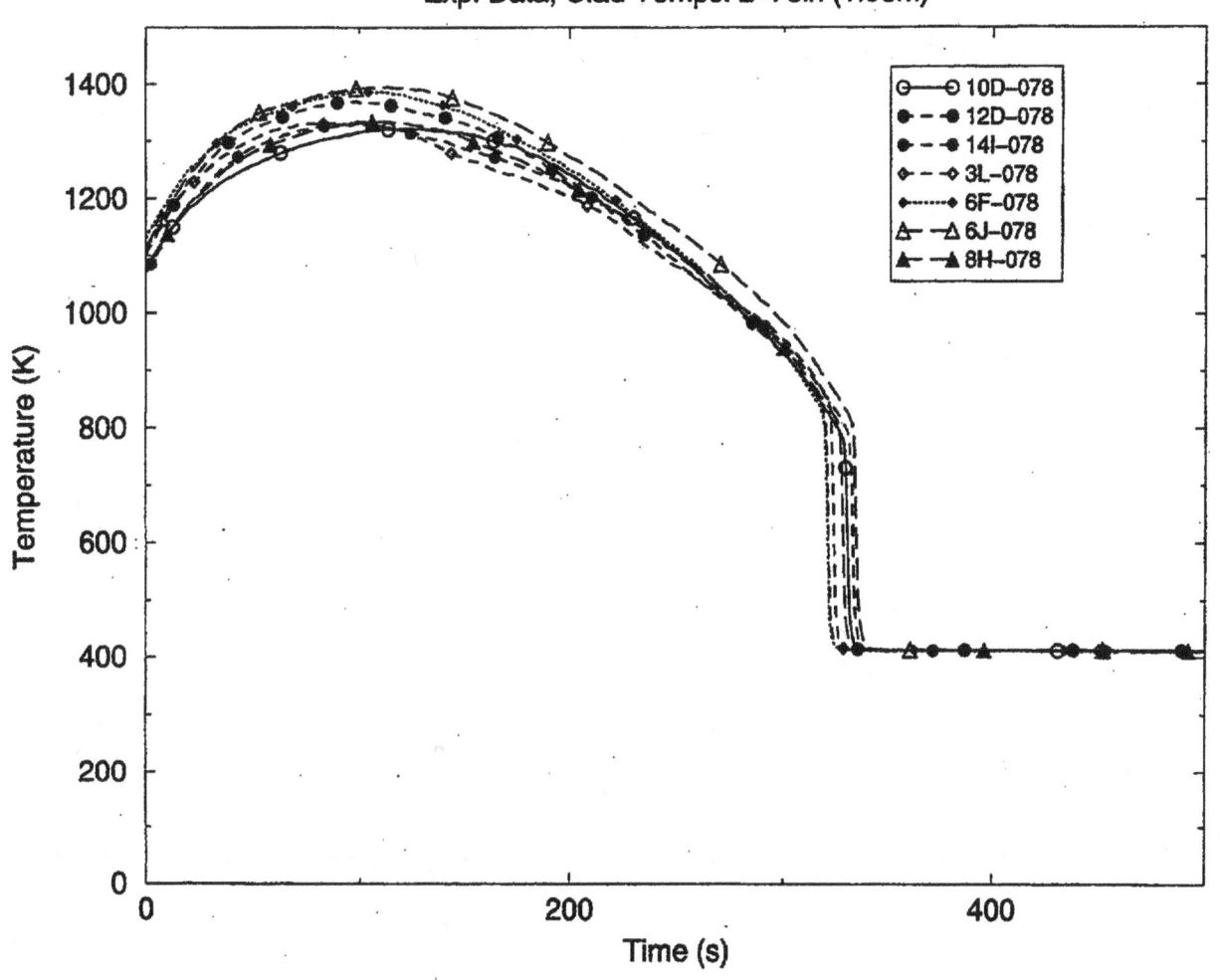

Figure 4.2 Flecht-Seaset 31504 Exp. Clad Temperatures, z=1.98m

Flecht–Seaset Forced Reflood 31504

Exp. Data. Clad Temps. z=102in (2.59m)–all data

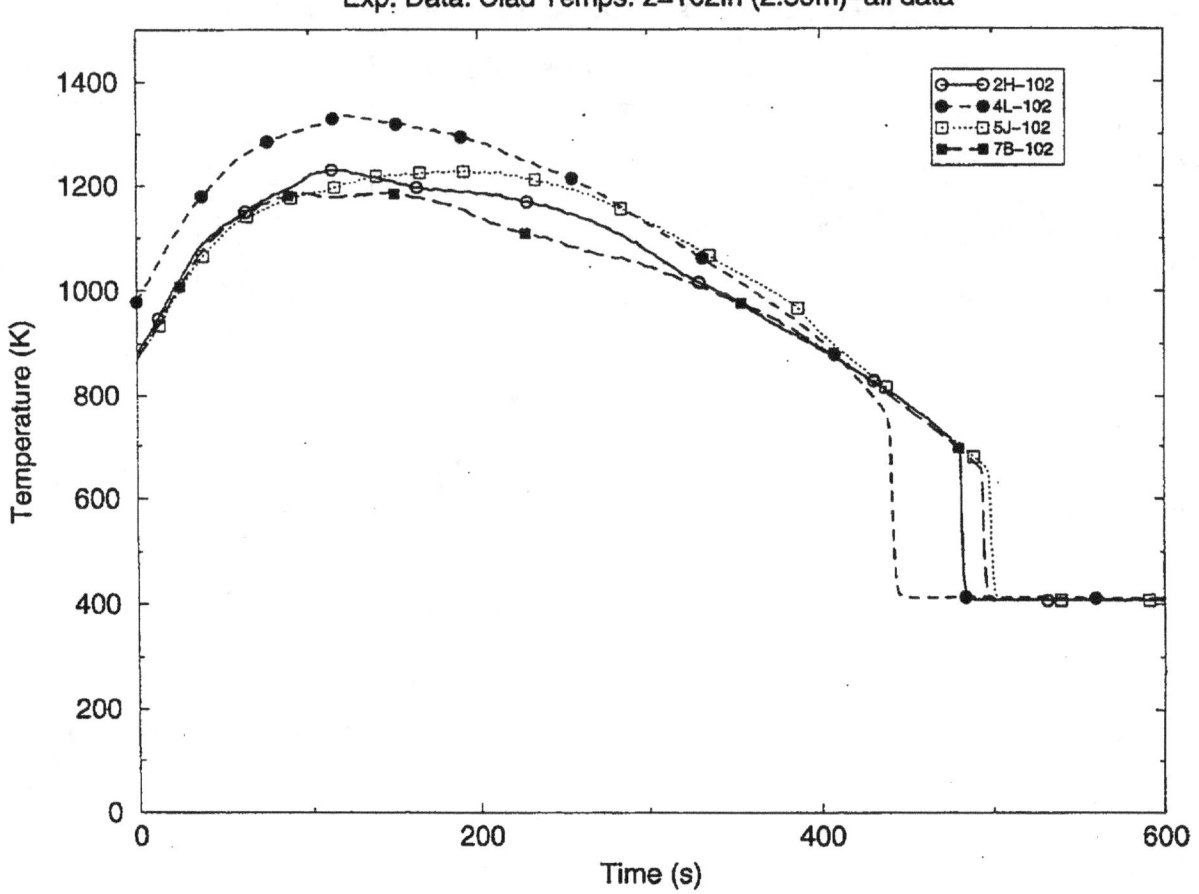

Figure 4.3 Flecht-Seaset 31504 Exp. Clad Temperatures, z=2.59m

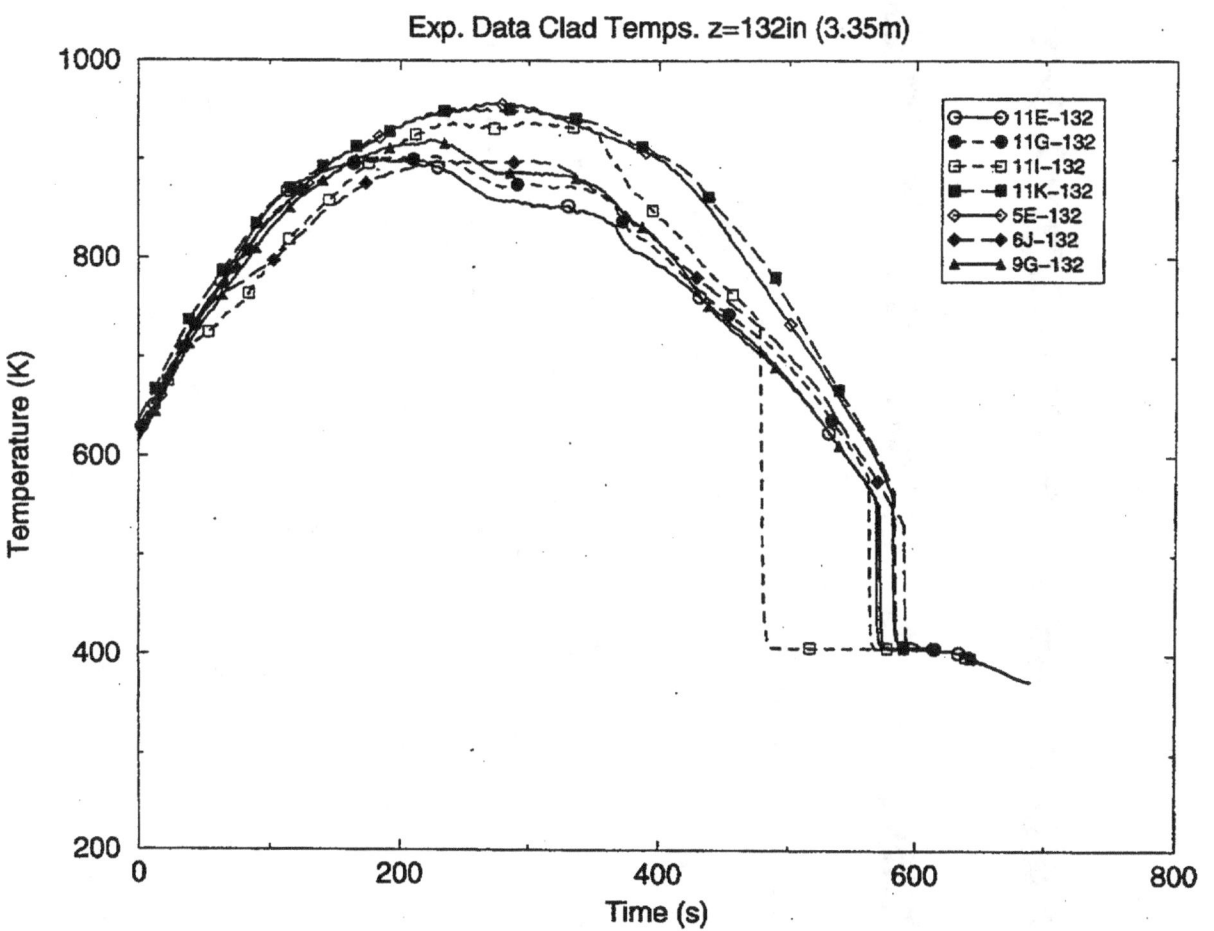

Figure 4.4 Flecht-Seaset 31504 Exp. Clad Temperatures, z=3.35m

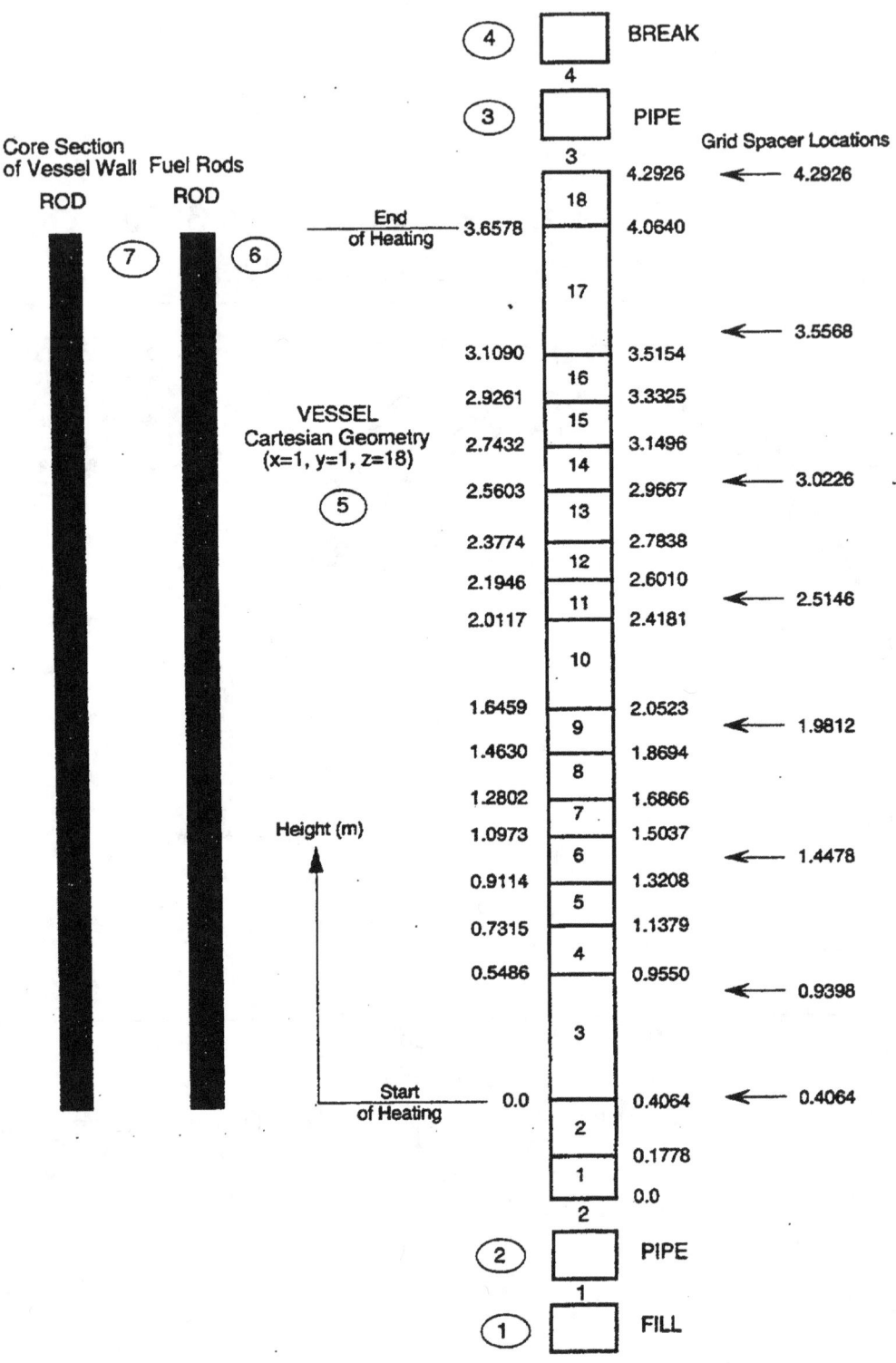

Figure 4.5 TRAC-M Input Model Schematic for Flecht-Seaset Run 31504

4.3 Comparison of TRAC-M(F90) and TRAC-M(F77) Calculations with Experimental Data from Flecht-Seaset Run 31504

Calculations were performed with TRAC-M(F77), Version 5.5.2A, and TRAC-M(F90), Version 3580. Both calculations used the newrfd=1 option, which specifies the bottom-up quenching reflood model developed in 1992. A top-down quenching model was added in 1999. In the TRAC-M(F77) code, if newrfd=3 is selected, this option will activate the combined model of bottom-up and top-down quenching. The TRAC-M(F90) code does not have this option. As stated earlier, the grid spacers are not modeled, and the expected uncertainty in predicting clad temperatures is on the order of 200 K.

Flecht-Seaset Run 31504 is one of a series of forced reflood tests conducted in the facility. Initial test conditions and key results from the test are presented in Table 1.

TABLE 1

CONDITIONS AND KEY RESULTS FOR RUN 31504

Parameter	Test Condition Value
Upper Plenum Pressure	0.28 MPa
Rod Initial Clad Temperature at the 1.83-m Level	1136 K
Rod Peak Power	2.3 kW/m
ECCS Injection Rate	~0.37 kg/s
Coolant Temperature	324 K
Radial Power Distribution	Uniform
Initial Temperature of Hottest Rod	1093 K
Elevation of Maximum Temperature of Hottest Rod	1.98 m
Maximum Temperature of Hottest Rod	1423 K
Temperature Rise	330 K
Turnaround Time of Hottest Rod	130 s
Quench Time of Hottest Rod	325 s
Bundle Quench Time	594 s

The input deck reflects the initial conditions reasonably well. A run following the experimental procedure; i.e., with application of a constant power without any inlet flow, has been performed. The rod surface temperature and steam temperature profiles were determined as the rod surface temperature at the location of the maximum heat generation reached the specified value at which the inlet flow and power decay would be initiated during experiments. These calculated temperature profiles were used as an input to the second deck to simulate initial test conditions. Figures 4.6 and 4.7 compare the calculated initial heater rod cladding and steam temperatures along the test section with experimental data, respectively. Calculated temperatures agree with experimental data very well.

The uncertainty of experimental measurements was on the order of 100 K in a two-phase flow. Experimental data shown in Figure 4.6 include all thermocouples including those giving erroneous readings. The data spread seems to be larger than 100 K. (It is on the order of 150 K.) One reading that seems to be an outlier can be thrown out. The data spread is probably attributable to natural circulation of the steam before the initiation of testing. Natural circulation would occur because of heat losses from the test section wall, and nonuniformity of the axial power shape. This is also substantiated in Figure 4.7, which depicts the initial axial variation of steam temperatures. The spread of experimental data is on the order of 100 to 150 K, and there is an outlier that can be thrown out. Calculations were performed using a one-dimensional model where the natural circulation is not modeled. Considering this limitation, the agreement between the calculated temperatures and measured data is Excellent for initial conditions.

The test was initiated by applying the decay power and forcing the specified inlet flow simulating the ECCS injection into the test section when the rod temperature reached the specified level. The test section was initially full of steam. As the inlet flow progressed, water slugs and droplets provided precursory cooling to the rods. As the flow progressed, the rods were quenched. Comparisons of calculated clad temperatures and experimental data are illustrated at different elevations of the test section in Figures 4.8 through 4.11. Clad temperatures are calculated with both TRAC-M(F77) and TRAC-M(F90) codes. Only bounding experimental temperature curves are shown. At t=0.0, the clad temperatures are at their initial values.

At a specified elevation

Temperatures initially increase because precursory cooling is not sufficient to immediately cool down the rods. As the time progresses, the quench front propagates, precursory cooling increases, and decay power and rod power decrease. If an elevation is specified, clad temperatures first increase, attain their maximum values, turn around as precursory cooling increases, and finally drop to saturation value as the rod quenches. Figure 4.12 illustrates the quench front propagation. Predictions of the quench time with the TRAC-M(F77) code during the first 200 s of the transient are slightly delayed, but they meet the acceptance criterion of 120 s spread. After 200 s, but before 500 s, predictions indicate substantially earlier quench that does not meet the acceptance criterion. Between 500 and 620 s, quenching occurs within the acceptance criterion. Predictions of the quench time with the TRAC-M(F90) code are always delayed. Except for the short time period in the beginning of the transient (about the first 150 s of the transient), the delay is beyond the acceptance criterion.

Figures 4.8 through 4.11 illustrate clad temperature predictions with both codes and bounding experimental data for various elevations of the test section. The bounding experimental data traces bound the spread of the experimental data, which is 100 K. Since the tests were run with grid spacers, and they are not modeled in the codes, the codes should predict hotter temperatures, up to 100 K, which is the expected bias. Figures 4.8 through 4.11 show that the predictions of maximum clad temperatures with the TRAC-M(F77) code meet the acceptance criterion for all elevations. Predictions with the TRAC-M(F90) code meet the acceptance criterion for low elevations (below ~2.00 m), but at higher elevations, they do not meet the acceptance criterion.

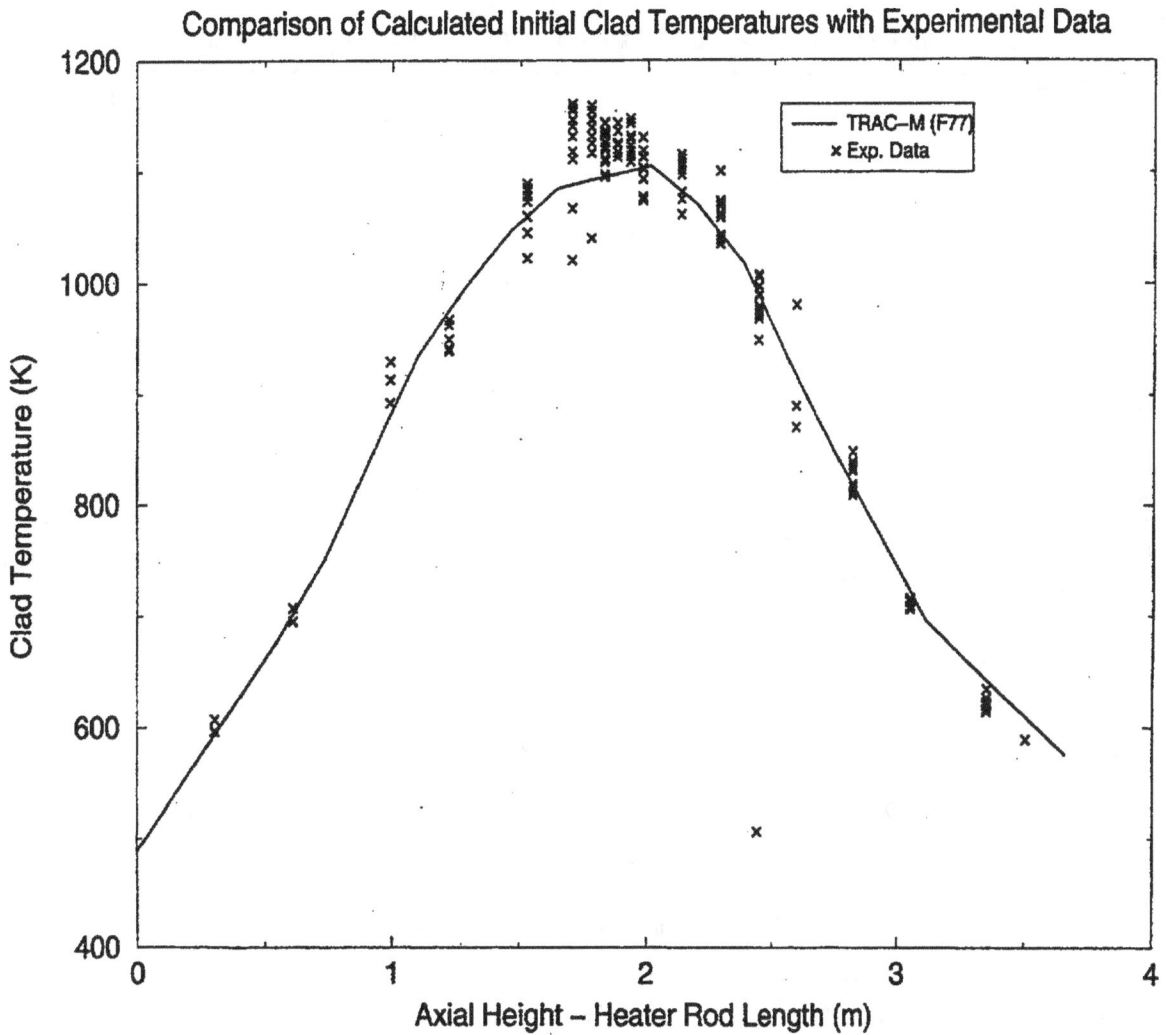

Figure 4.6 Initial Axial Clad Temperature Variation

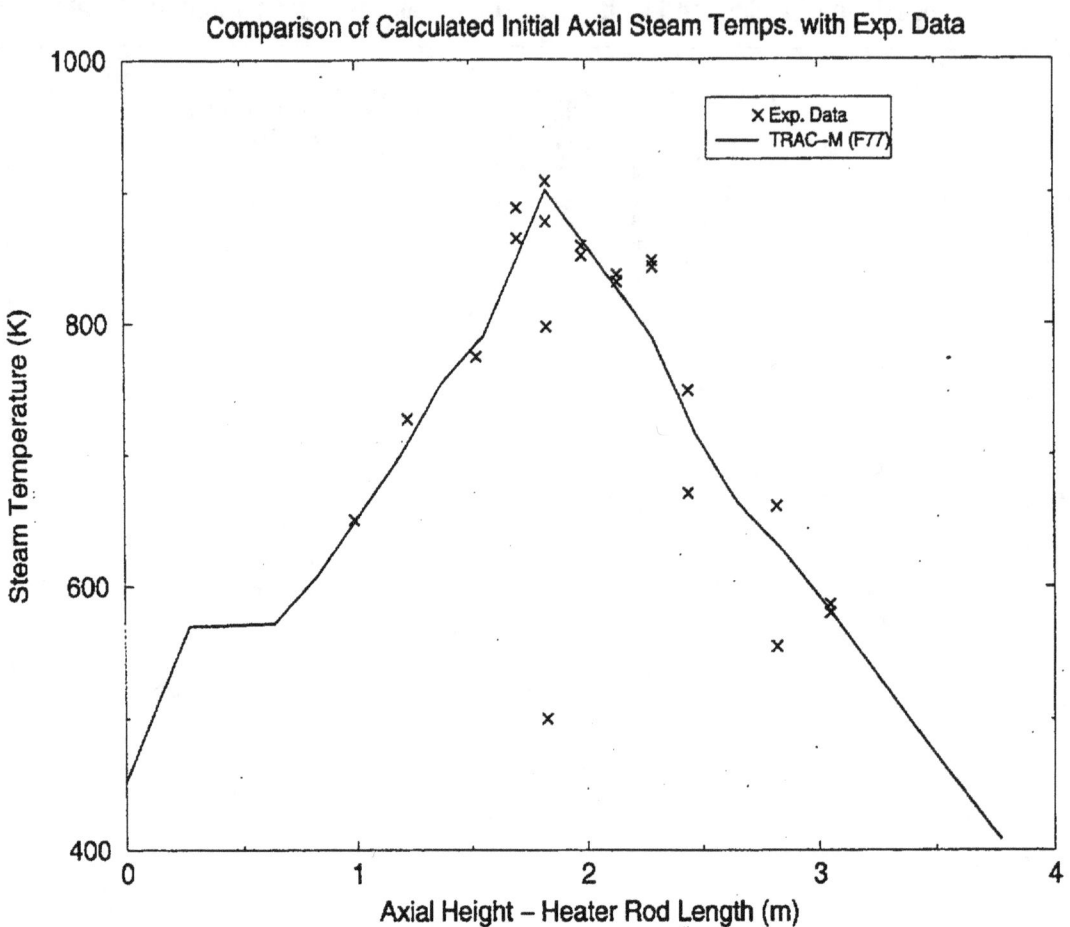

Figure 4.7 Initial Axial Steam Temperature Variation

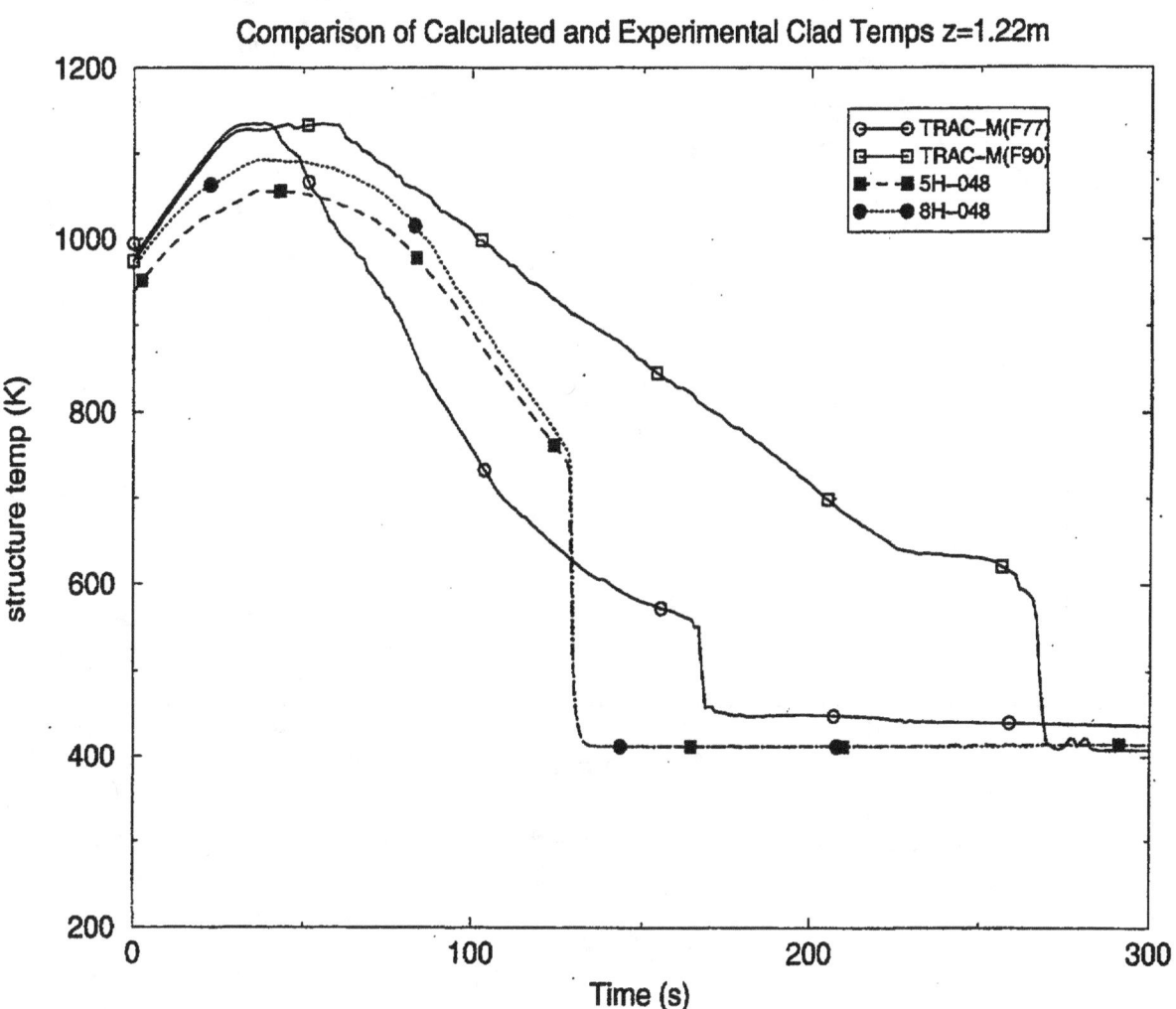

Figure 4.8 Comparison of Calculated and Experimental Clad Temps.
@z=1.22m

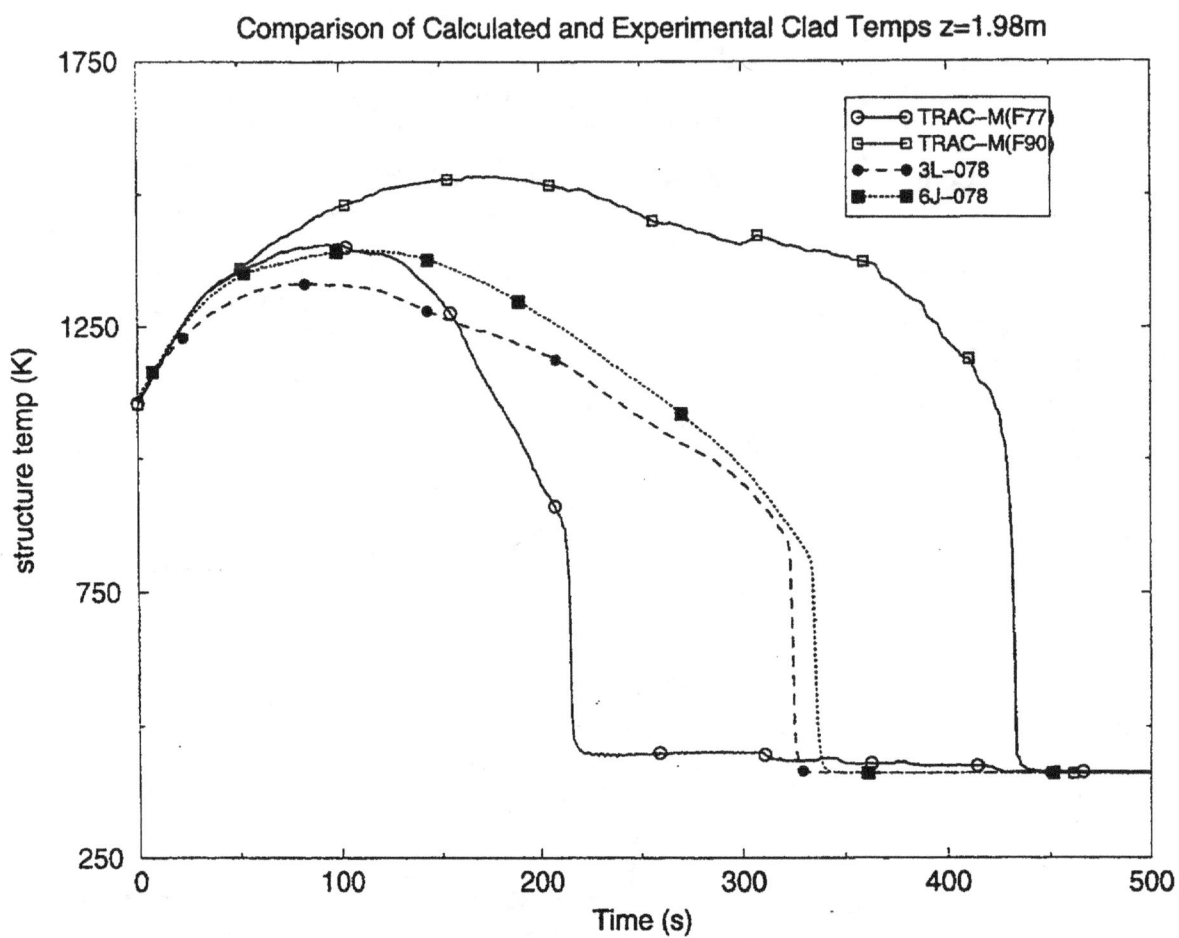

Figure 4.9 Comparison of Calculated and Experimental Clad Temps.
@z=1.98m

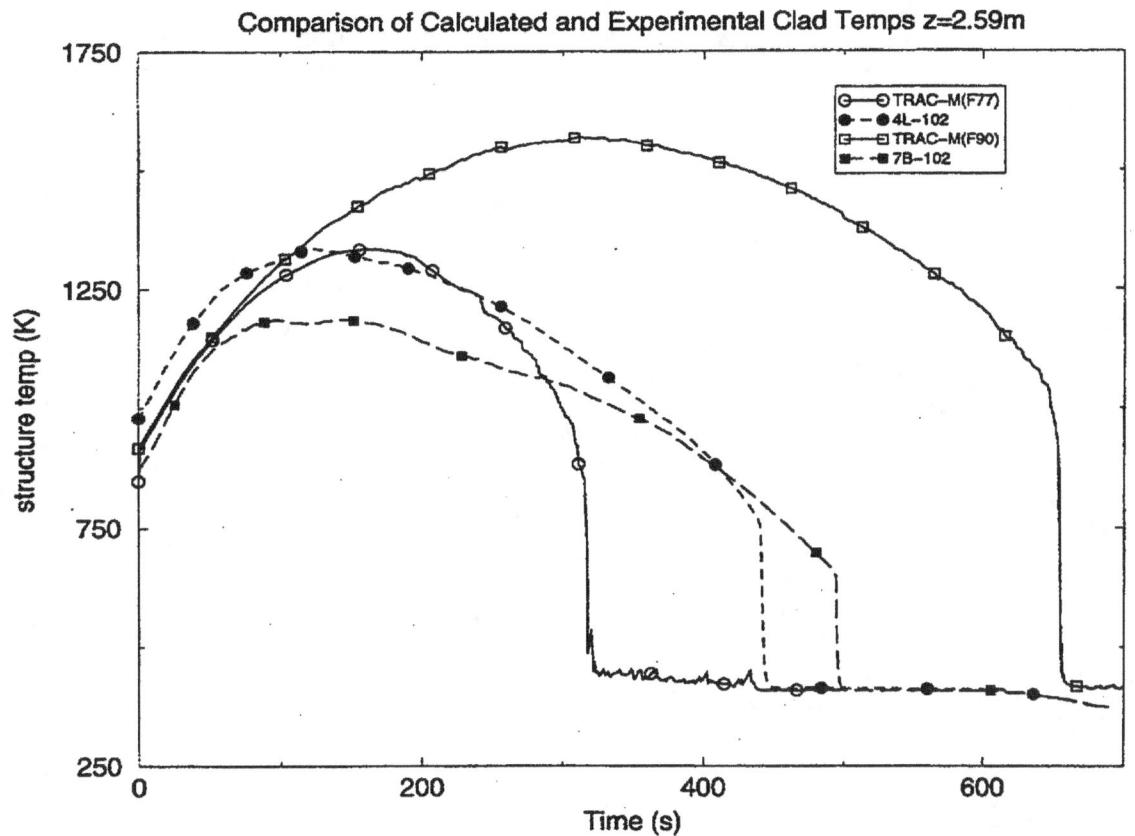

Figure 4.10 Comparison of Calculated and Experimental Clad Temps.
@z=2.59m

Flecht–Seaset Forced Reflood 31504

Comparison of Calculated and Experimental Clad Temps z=3.35m

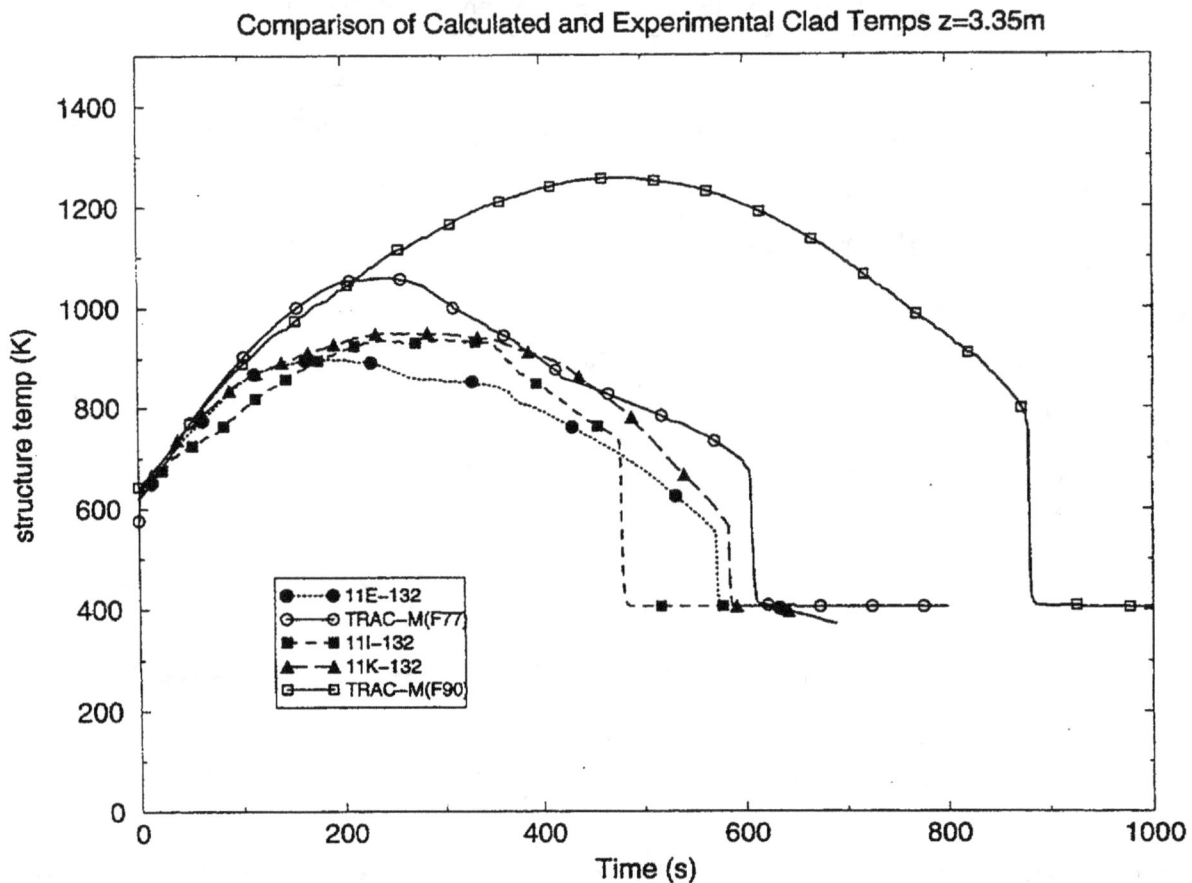

Figure 4.11 Comparison of Calculated and Experimental Clad Temps.
@z=3.35m

Flecht Seaset Forced Reflood 31504

Comparison of Calculated and Experimental Quench Elevations

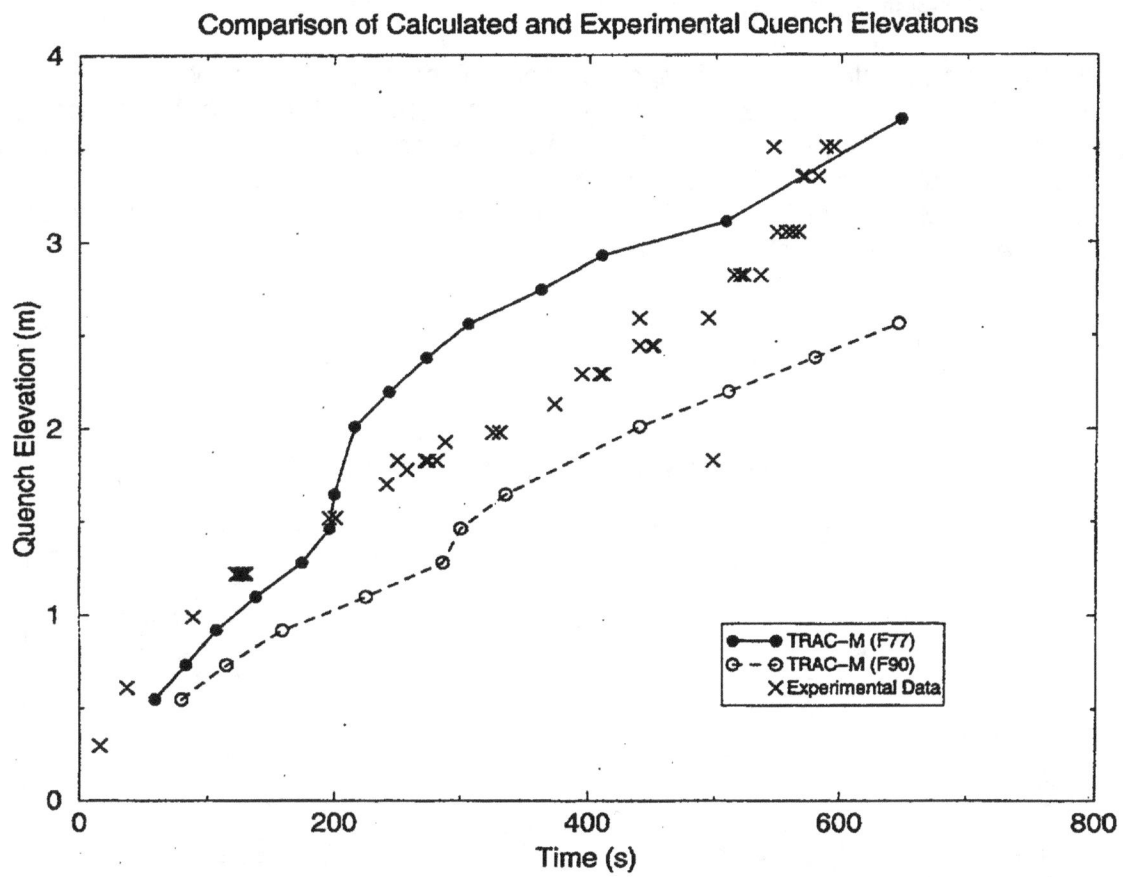

Figure 4.12 Calculated and Measured Quench Front Propagation

Figure 4.13 illustrates experimental differential pressure data taken along the test section. These data were taken at 1-foot increments starting from the 0-foot reference and ending at the 10-foot height. Observe that the data indicate orderly and monotonic progression of a sharp quench front suggested by rapid increases of pressure drops at lower elevations, from 0 to 4 feet. The sharpness of the quench front disappears at higher elevations; however, progression of the quench front is still orderly and monotonic; i.e., the height of the quench front increases with increasing time.

Figure 4.14 illustrates calculations of vapor fractions along axial distance with the TRAC-M(F77) code. Although calculations show predictions of quench fronts at different times, they indicate that progression is not orderly and monotonic; e.g., quenching at lower elevations occurs at later times. Calculations and animation of the results with the XTV code show that the quench front and vapor fractions along the test section continuously oscillate. This shows that the code does not correctly predict the phenomena.

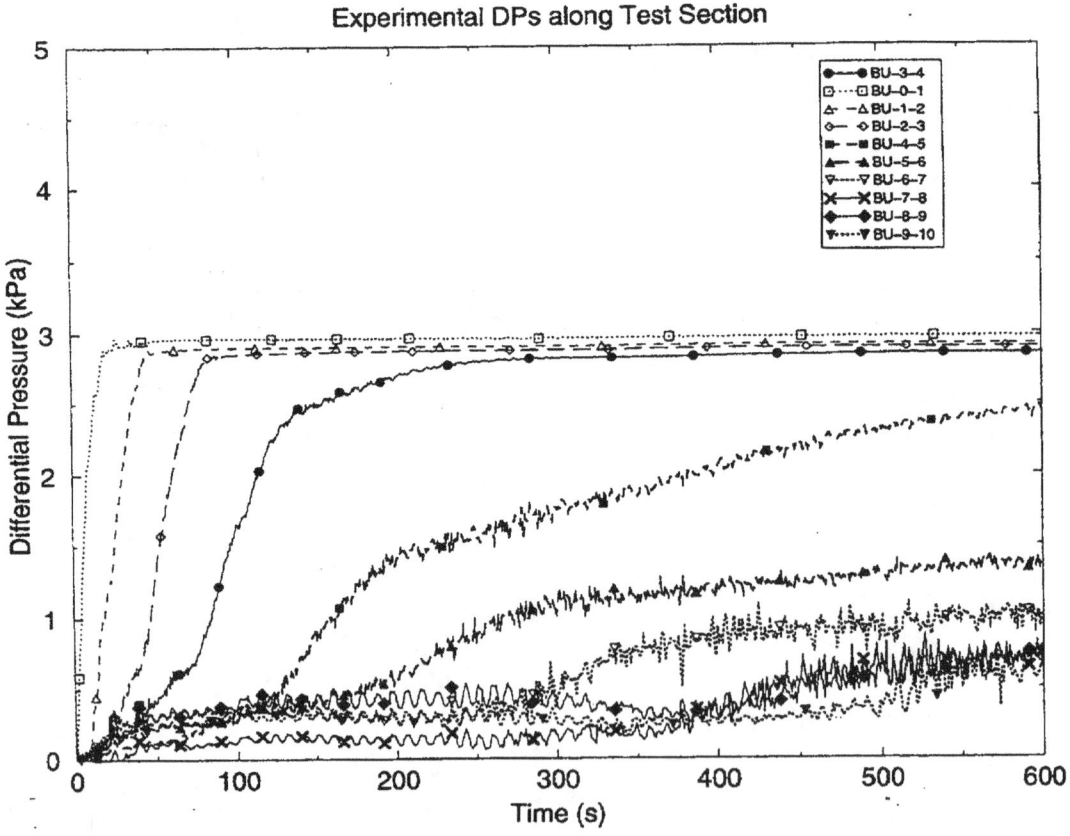

Figure 4.13 Experimental Differential Pressure
Measurements Along the Test Section

Flecht Seaset Forced Reflood 31504

Calculated Axial Void Fraction Distribution at Different Times

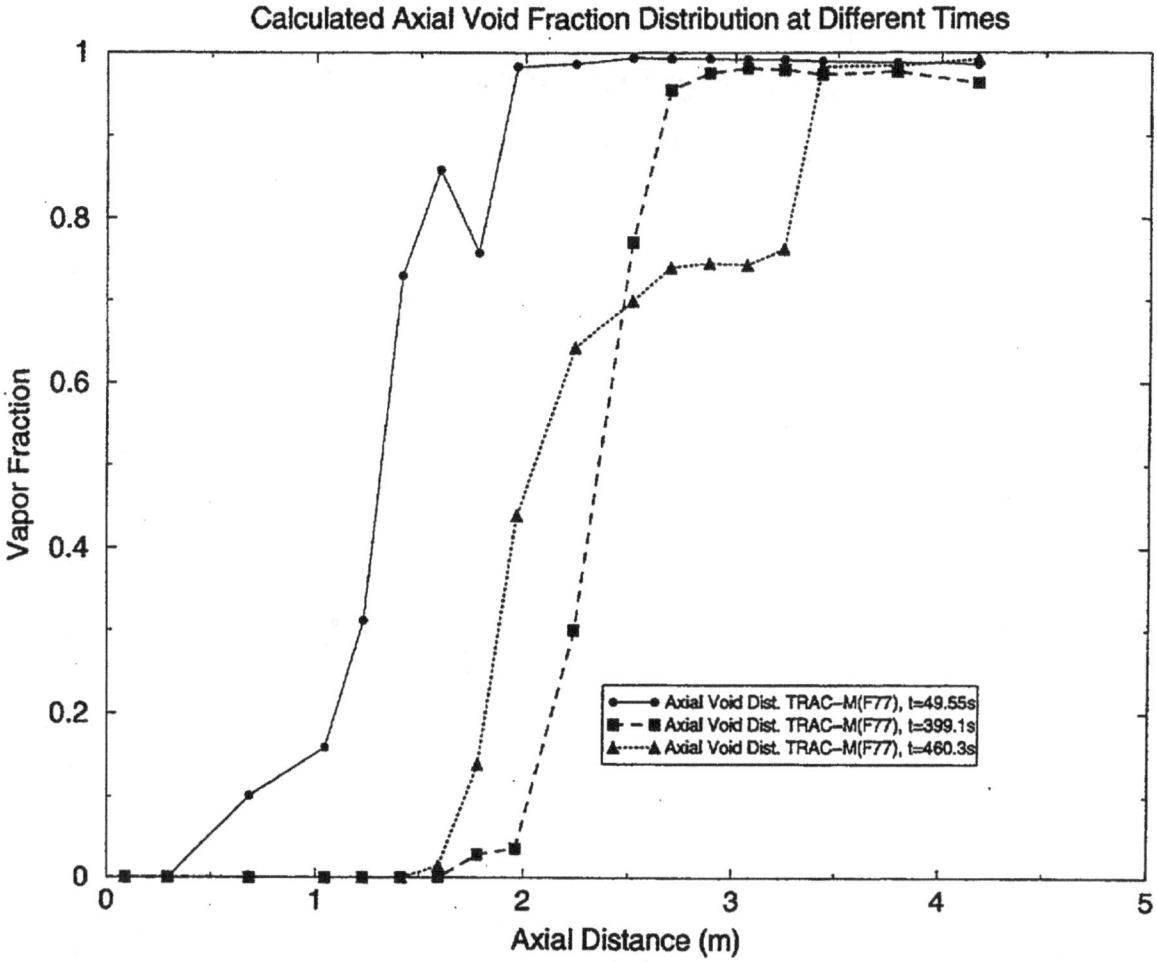

Figure 4.14 Calculation of Axial Void Fraction Distribution by
TRAC-M(F77) Code

Figures 4.15 through 4.20 present comparisons of code predictions of differential pressure drops with experimental data. Both codes predict large-amplitude, high-frequency oscillations, while the measurements show relatively smooth conditions. The predictions of large-amplitude, high-frequency oscillations are not considered realistic. Qualitatively, there is "Insufficient agreement" between the calculations and test data.

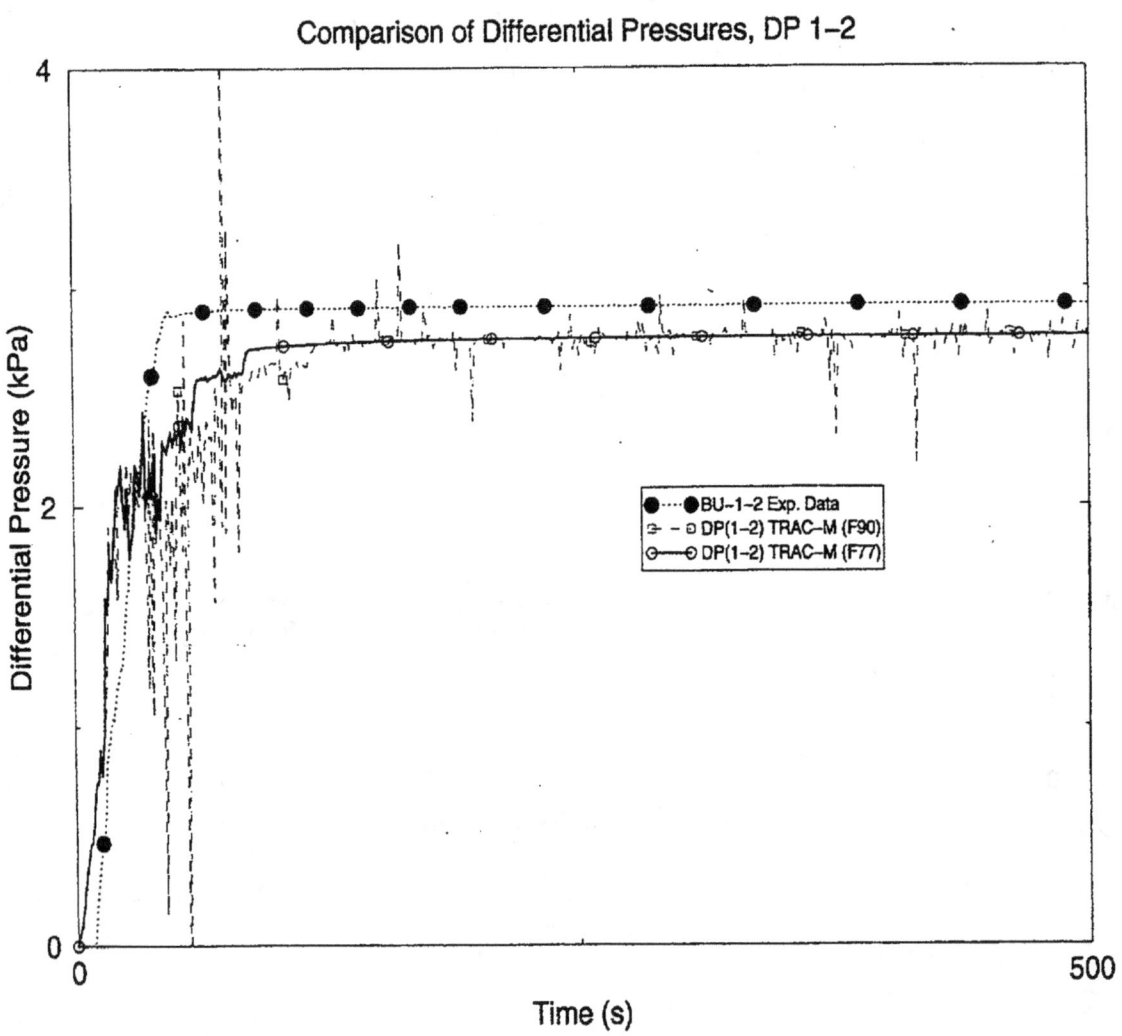

Figure 4.15 Comparison of Differential Pressures (Taps 1 - 2)

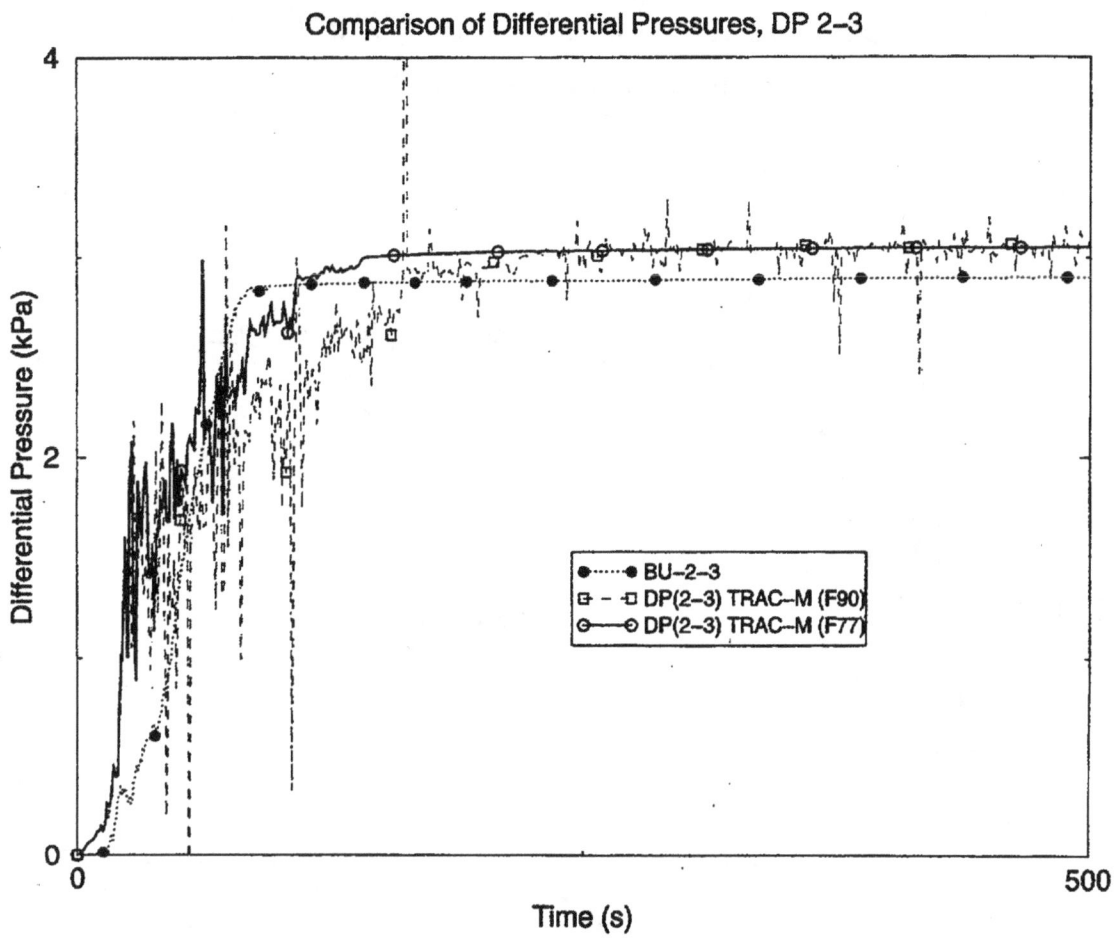

Figure 4.16 Comparison of Differential Pressures (Taps 2 - 3)

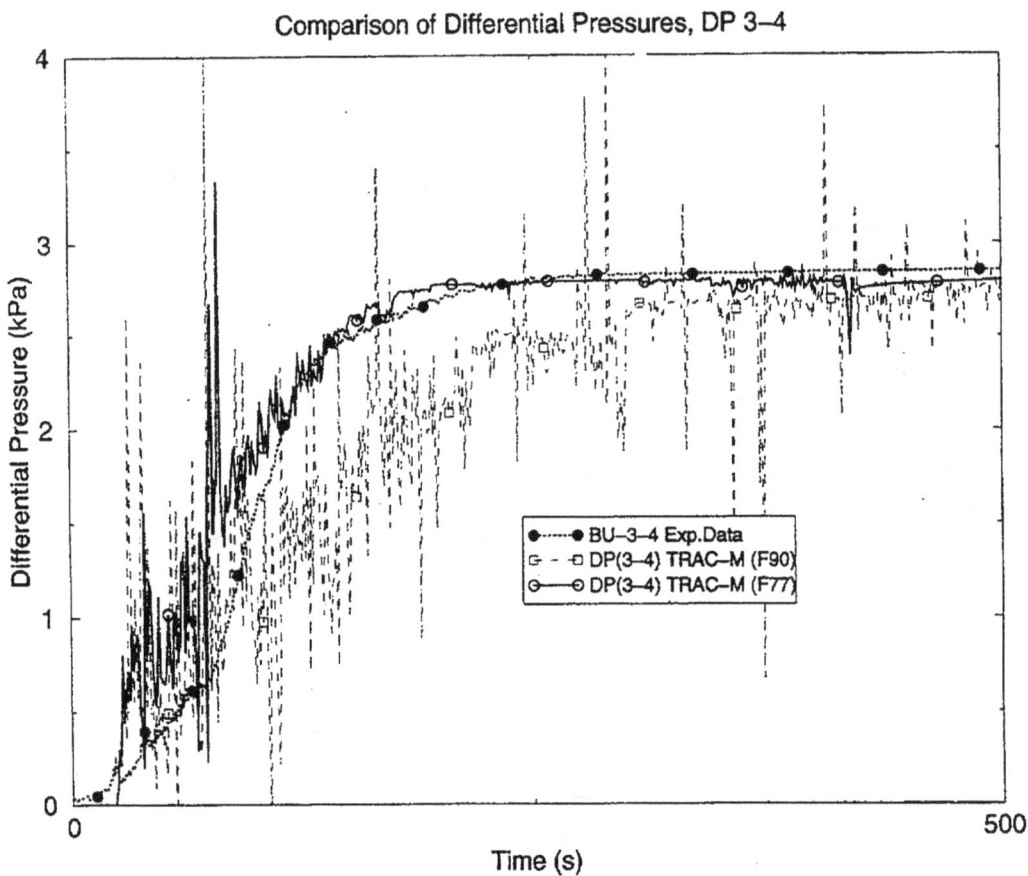

Figure 4.17 Comparison of Differential Pressures (Taps 3 - 4)

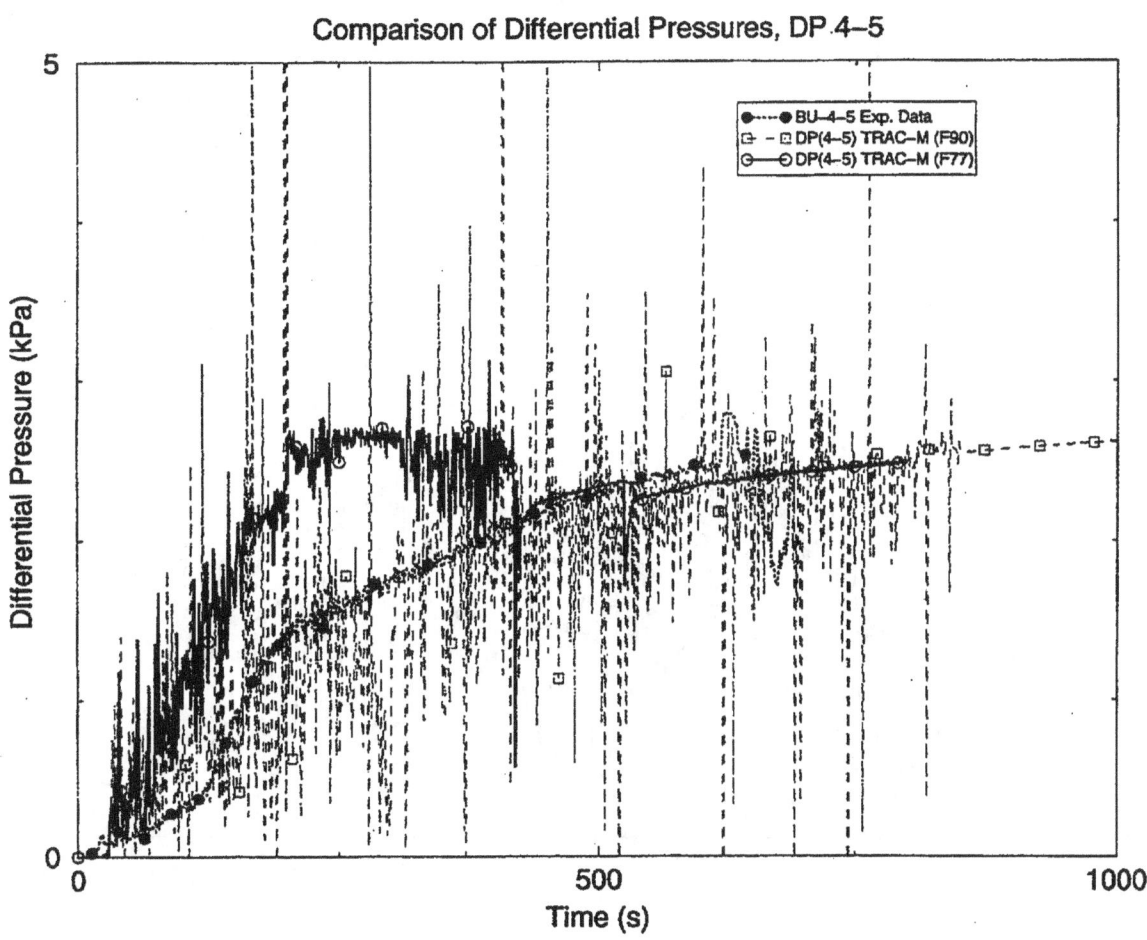

Figure 4.18 Comparison of Differential Pressures (Taps 4 - 5)

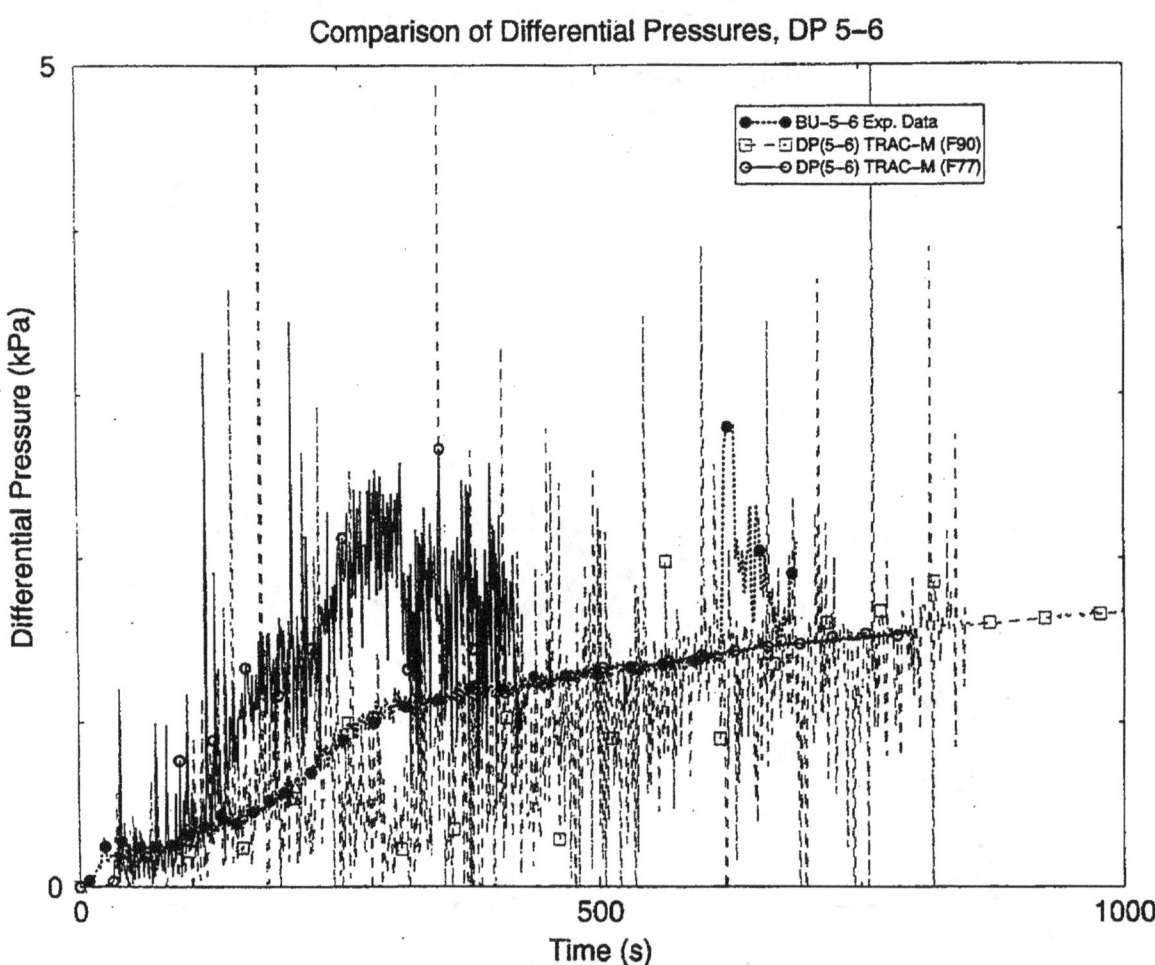

Figure 4.19 Comparison of Differential Pressures (Taps 5 - 6)

Flecht–Seaset Forced Reflood 31504

Comparison of Differential Pressures, DP 6–7

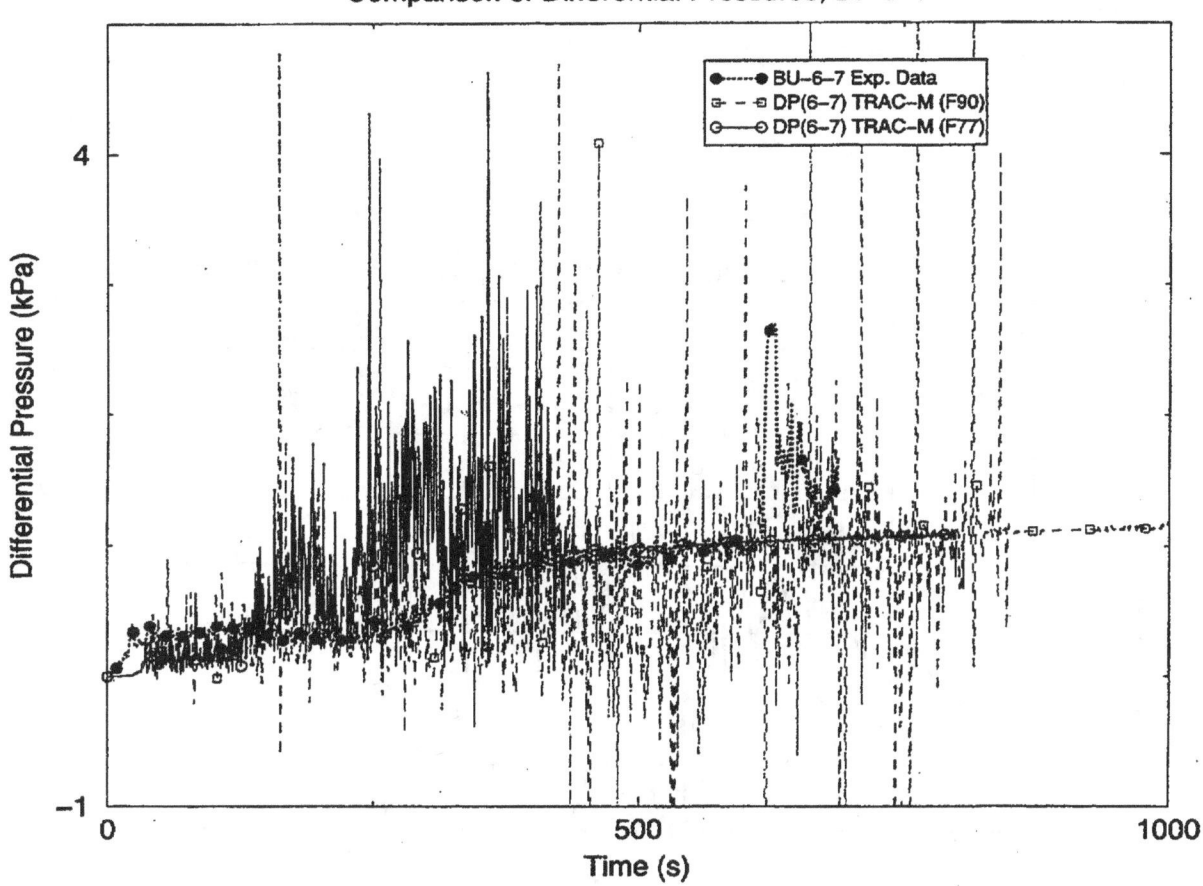

Figure 4.20 Comparison of Differential Pressures (Taps 6 - 7)

Figures 4.21 through 4.23 present comparison of calculated steam temperatures with experimental data at some elevations. There are very few steam temperature measurements; hence, an estimate of their uncertainties cannot be made. However, comparisons indicate that calculated values differ by several hundred degrees from the experimental data. Hence, the agreement is Insufficient.

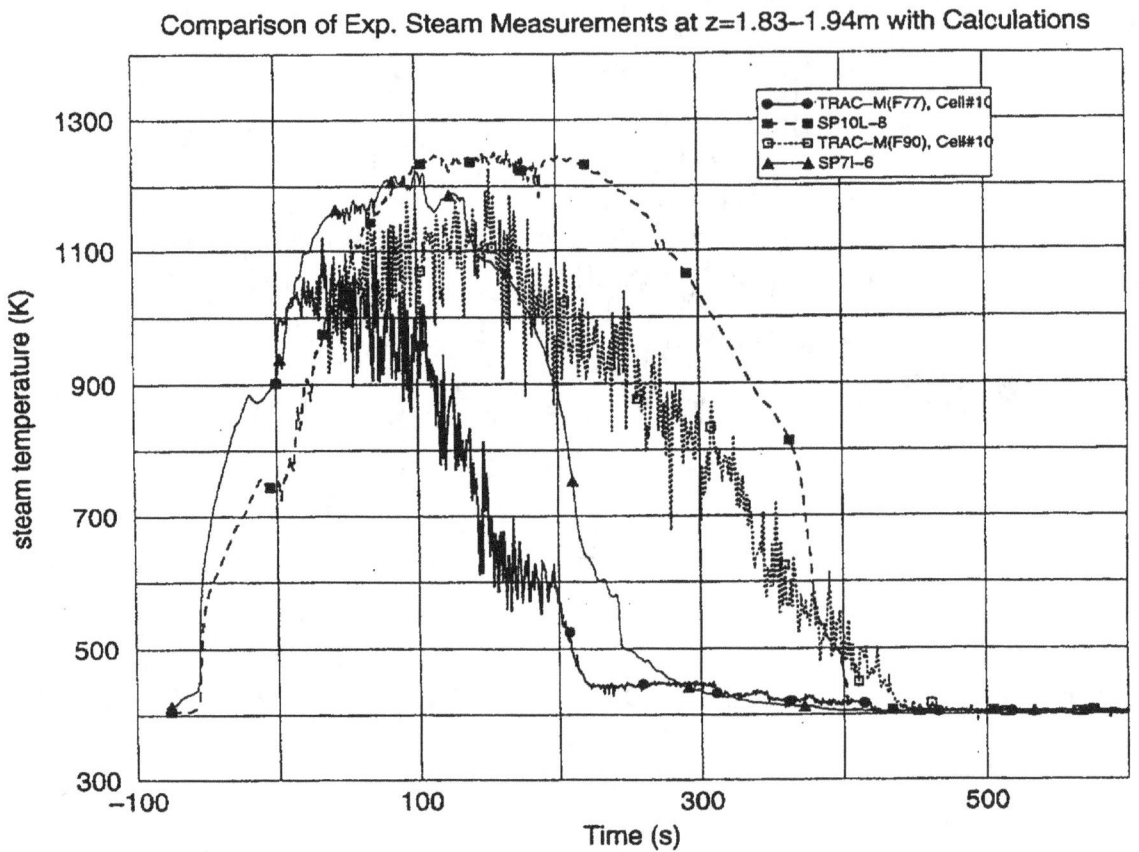

Flecht–Seaset Forced Reflood 31504
Comparison of Exp. Steam Measurements at z=1.83–1.94m with Calculations

Figure 4.21 Steam Temperatures (Z=1.83 – 1.94m)

Flecht–Seaset Forced Reflood 31504

Comparison of Exp. Steam Measurements at z=2.82–3.05m with Calculations

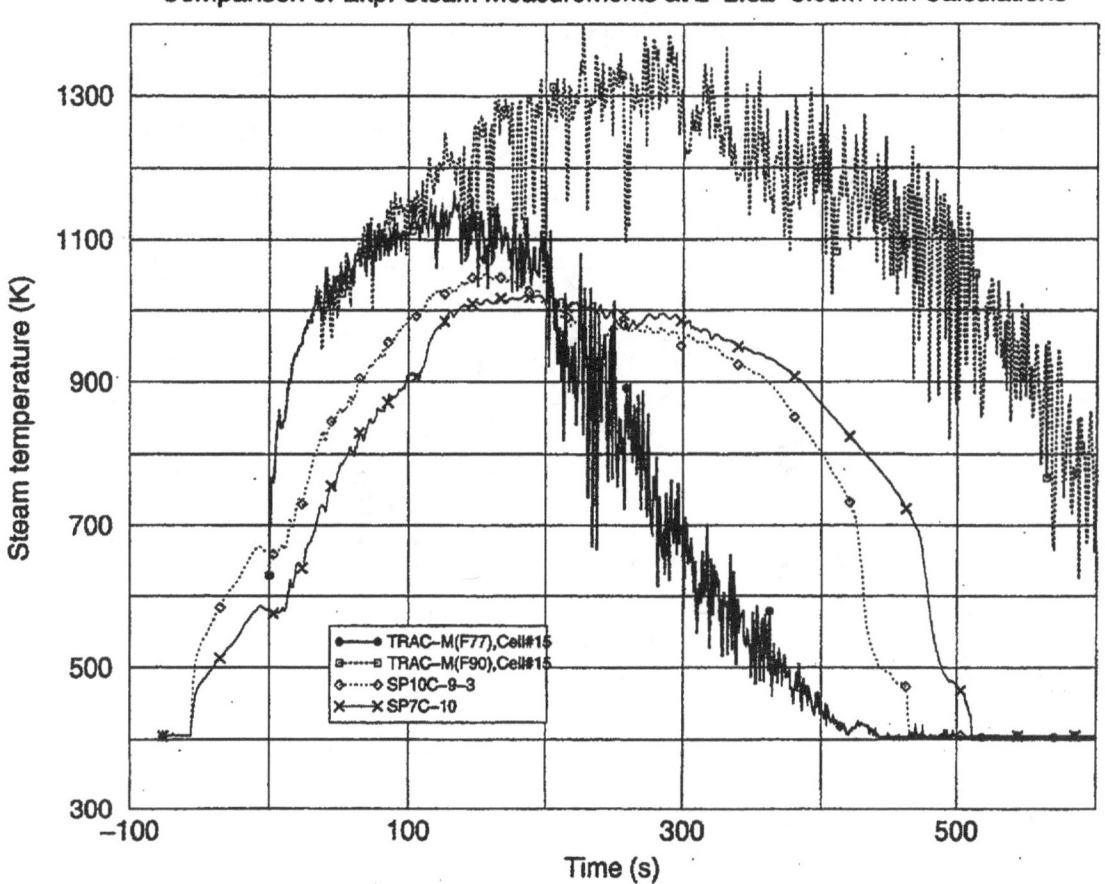

Figure 4.22 Steam Temperatures (Z=2.82 - 3.03m)

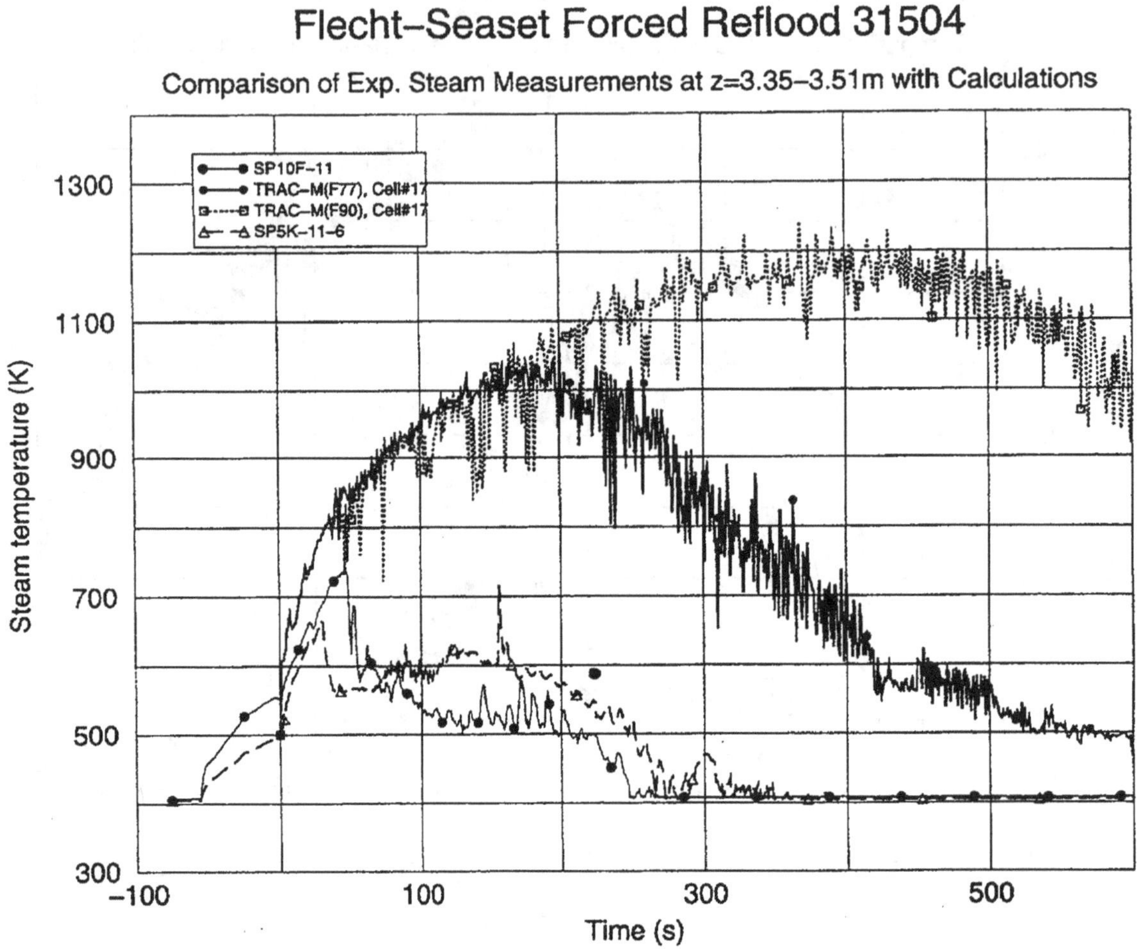
Flecht–Seaset Forced Reflood 31504
Comparison of Exp. Steam Measurements at z=3.35–3.51m with Calculations
SP10F–11
TRAC–M(F77), Cell#17
TRAC–M(F90), Cell#17
SP5K–11–6
1300
1100
900
700
500
300
Steam temperature (K)
–100
100
300
500
Time (s)

Figure 4.23 Steam Temperatures (Z=3.35 - 3.51m)

These comparisons indicate that the codes are not correctly predicting phenomena. Although peak clad temperature predictions with the TRAC-M(F77) code are excellent, the rest of the clad temperature predictions Minimally agree with the data. There is Insufficient agreement between predictions of differential pressures and steam temperatures and test data. One can conclude that predictions of peak clad temperatures are fortuitous.

A big surprise in code calculations was that differences between TRAC-M(F77) and TRAC-M(F90) predictions were very high. Examination of output files indicated that the TRAC-M(F77) code was predicting choked flow at the exit of the test section. There were some corrections to the choked flow model in the TRAC-M(F90) code; therefore, the code was not predicting choked conditions. Figure 4.24 demonstrates the effects of choked flow predictions. The choking of the flow produces high pressures in the test section as predicted by the TRAC-M(F77), code while the prediction of the test section pressure with the TRAC-M(F90) code remains almost at a constant value of 40 psia (the pressure level at which the experiments were conducted).

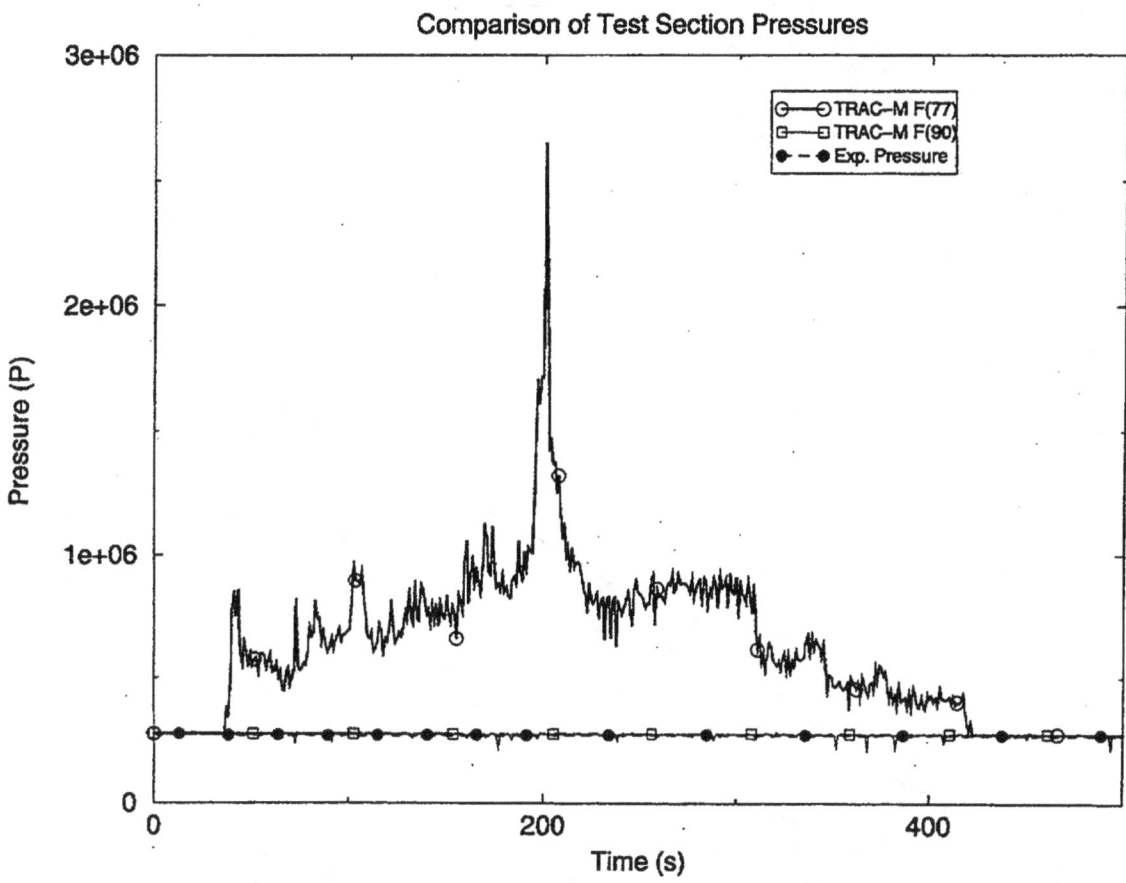

Figure 4.24 Comparison of Test Section Pressures

Choking should not have been predicted since this phenomenon does not occur during reflood. It is clear that the code predictions are completely wrong, and the codes are predicting different phenomena. Prediction of choking with the TRAC-M(F77) code indicates that predictions of two-phase velocities are also extremely high. Corrections of the choking model in the TRAC-M(F90) code does not change this conclusion. Since choking is not predicted in the TRAC-M(F90) code, prediction of two-phase velocities should be higher. It is expected that predictions with both codes would indicate substantially more liquid carryout than in testing. This would lead to higher clad temperature predictions, since less liquid would contact the surfaces of the rods and less cooling would occur. Figures 4.25 and 4.26 compare the predicted liquid and steam carryouts (integrated liquid and steam outflows) with experimental data.

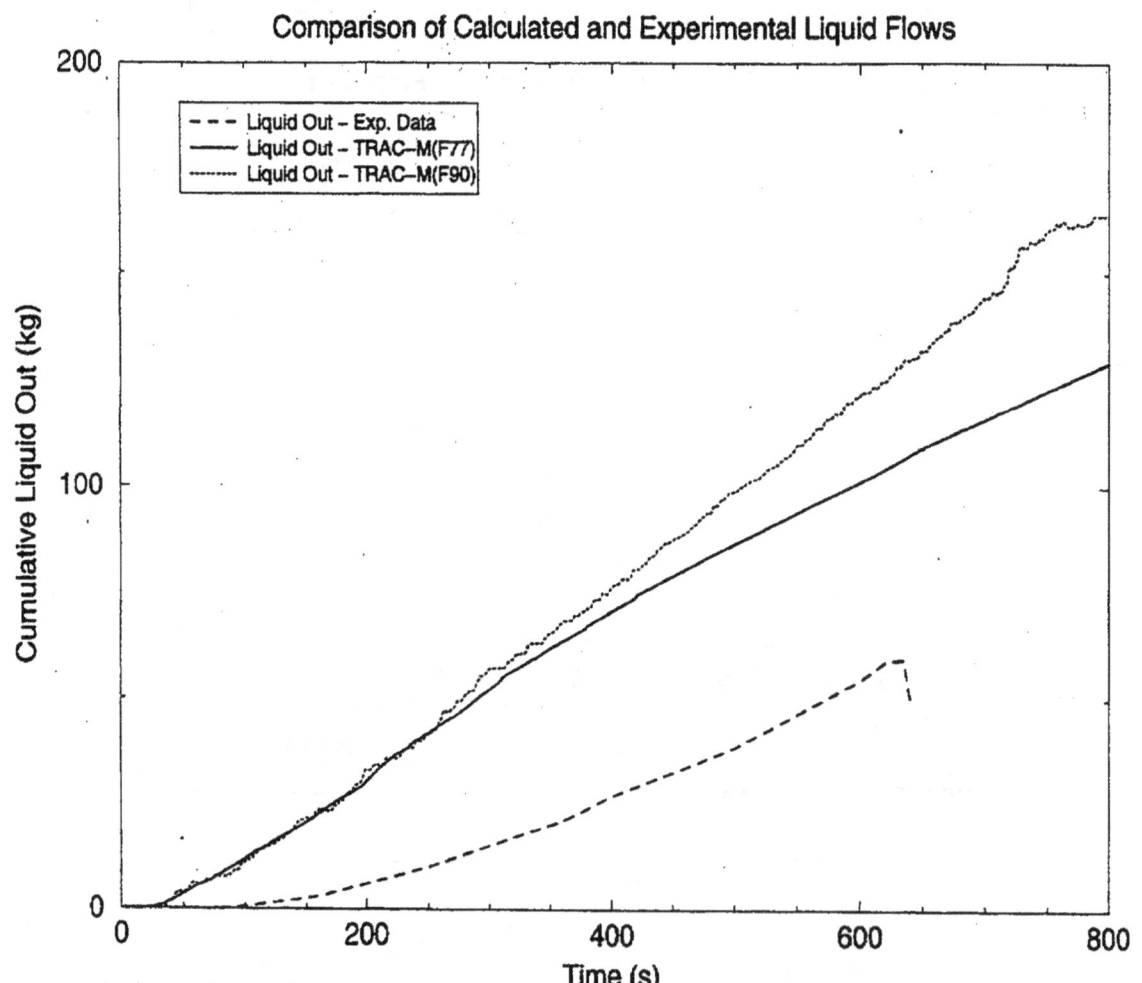

Figure 4.25 Comparison of Liquid Carryouts

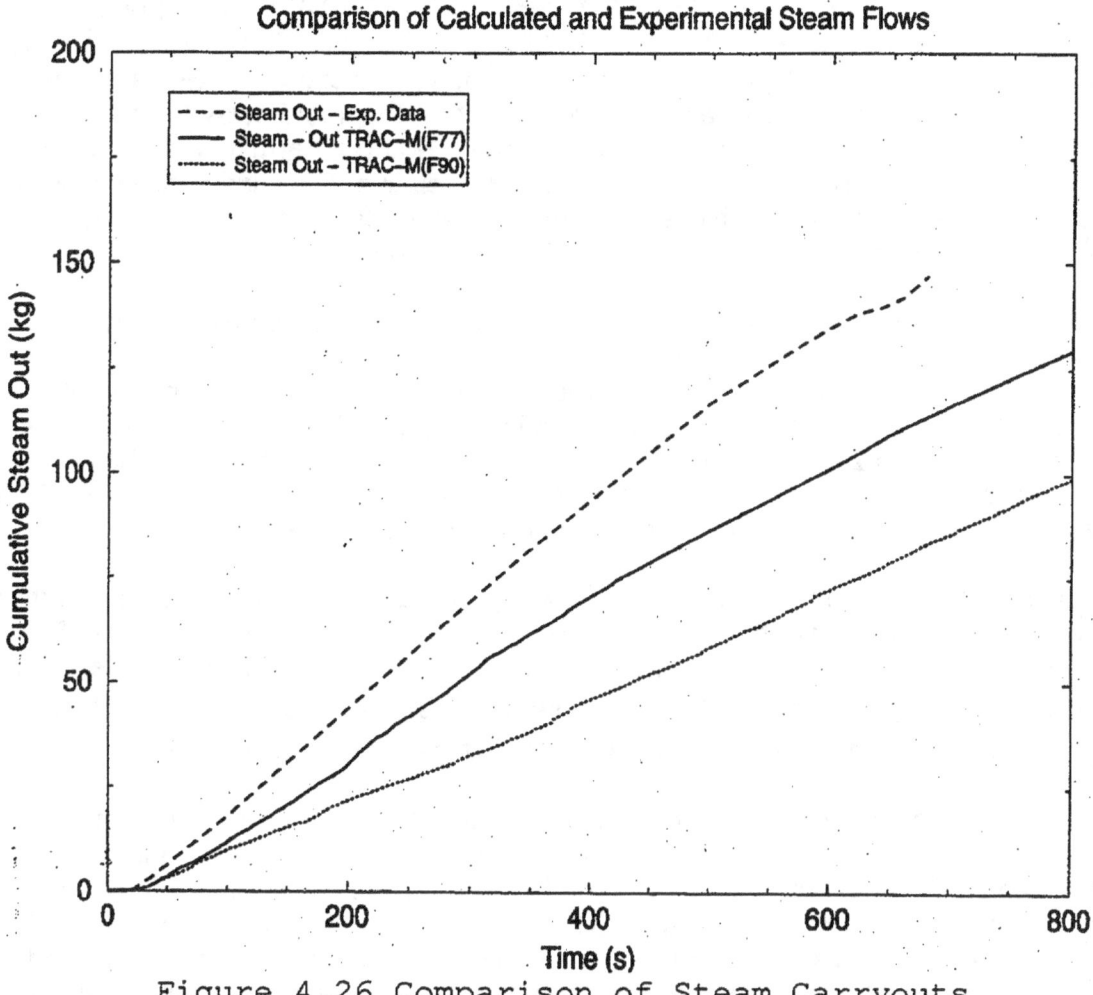

Figure 4.26 Comparison of Steam Carryouts

As expected, Figure 4.25 demonstrates predictions of excessive liquid carryout by both codes. Excessive liquid carryout leads to predictions of less energy removal and higher clad temperatures. It also leads to production of less steam than measured during experiments. This is confirmed in Figure 4.26.

4.4 Discussion of TRAC Models

Excessive liquid carryout has been predicted in many reflood tests (Ref. 15). Excessive liquid carryout is an indication that the interfacial area used by the code is larger than in tests. This raises the question of how well flow regime maps have been modeled in the code.

Figure 4.27 shows the flow regime map used in the TRAC code during reflood when the inlet conditions are subcooled or low quality. The flow regime map is an "Inverted Annular Flow" regime, which is also depicted in Figure 2.2. Figures 4.28 and 4.29 show the relative velocities calculated with TRAC-M(F77) and TRAC-M(F90) codes at Cell #10 (about at the middle of the test section) and at Cell #17 (almost at the end of the test section). Note that the relative velocities are very high. High steam velocities may tear the liquid away from the liquid core, and also carry large liquid slugs out of the test section without permitting the liquid to contact the heated walls for a sufficient length of time. High relative velocities explain why the liquid carryout from the test section is higher than the measured level, and why calculated clad temperatures are generally higher than experimental values.

The TRAC flow regime maps are predicated on the work performed by Ishii and his coworkers (Ref. 16). The reference indicates that these flow regime maps exist at relatively low relative velocities. For example, it states that if the relative velocity is increased to 2.0 m/s, smooth and rough wavy sections are nonexistent. The relative velocities shown in Figures 4.28 and 4.29 are much higher than 2.0 m/s. They go up to 20.0 m/s. This would lead to the conclusion that at these predicted velocities, flow regime maps used by the TRAC-M(F77) of TRAC-M(F90) codes cannot be consistent with the flow regimes that occurred in tests.

According to Ref. 16, the inverted annular flow regime has four different regions with distinct characteristics (smooth, rough-wavy, agitated flow, and dispersed flow regions). Figure 4.27 depicts these regions, as well as the transition flow region. This last region refers to the transition boiling region between the CHF point and the T_q. The tests in Ref. 16 were performed under conditions that did not simulate the transition flow region.

Ref. 16 defines boundaries for four different regions. A break-up length for each region is defined by a correlation. Each correlation is founded on the Capillary number, and has its own region of applicability, which is predicated on both the Weber number and the vapor fraction measured at the inlet of the test section. The Weber number is founded on the relative velocity between the liquid and gas. An examination of the documentation on the TRAC code (Ref. 17) indicates that although the same Ishii correlations for break-up lengths have been used, the same regions of applicability have not been used. The code uses different regions of applicability that are defined by the vapor fraction alone, and are not predicated on the Weber number. Table 2, below, shows the Capillary number criteria and the Weber number restrictions in Ref. 16 and TRAC code application in Ref. 17.

In Ref. 16 Z is the average break up length measured from the inlet of the test section, D is the liquid jet hole diameter, Ca is the Capillary number defined using fluid jet properties (viscosity, velocity and surface tension) at the inlet, $Ca = \mu_l V_l / \sigma_l$, We is the Weber number defined using fluid jet and gas properties at the inlet, $We = \rho \left(V_g - V_l \right)^2 D / \sigma_l$, and α_i is the void fraction at the inlet of the test section.

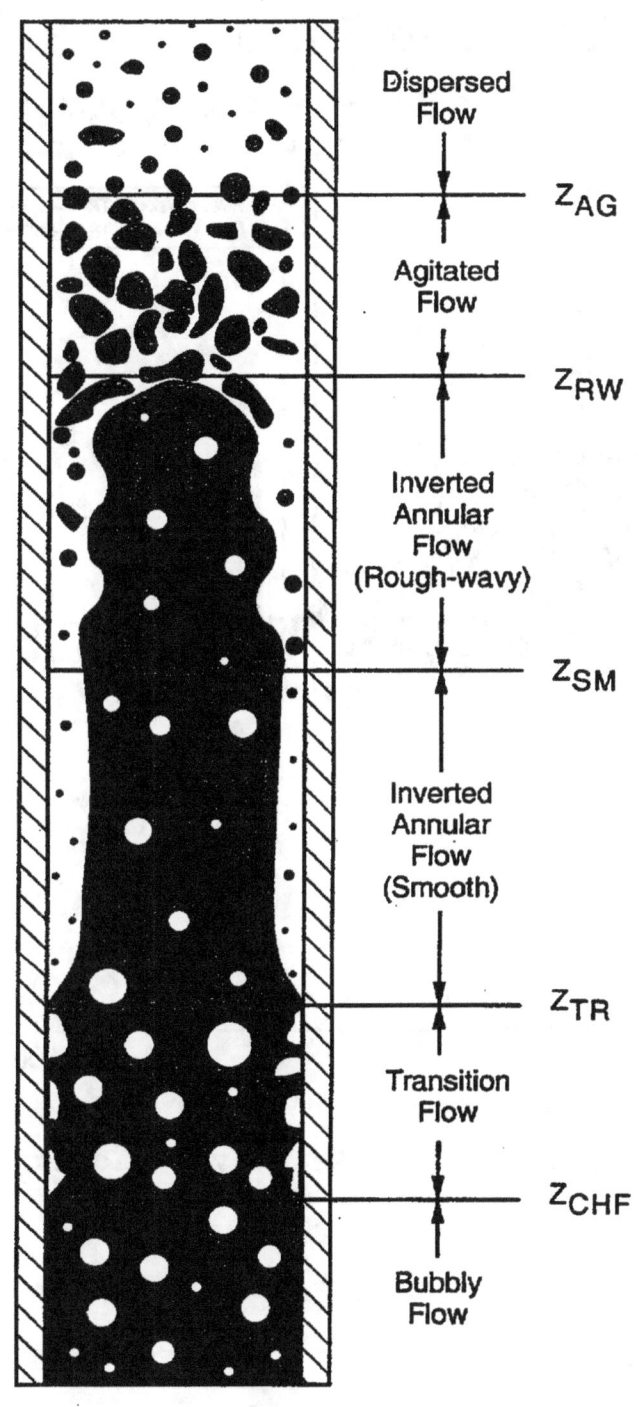

Figure 4.27 TRAC-M Reflood Flow
Regime Map

Flecht Seaset Forced Reflood 31504

Comparison of Relative Velocities, (Vg–Vl), at Cell#10

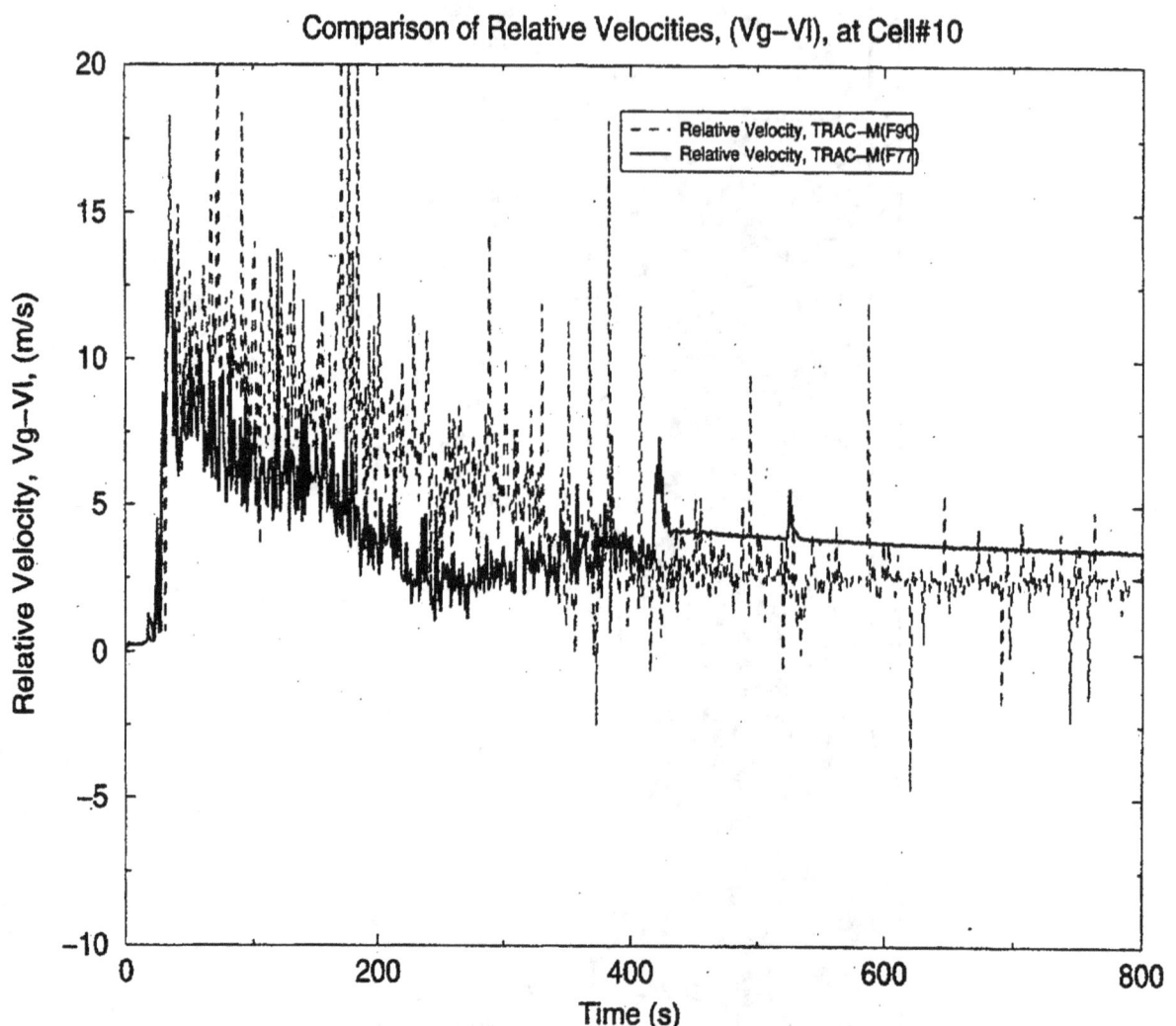

Figure 4.28 Calculated Relative Velocities at Cell #10

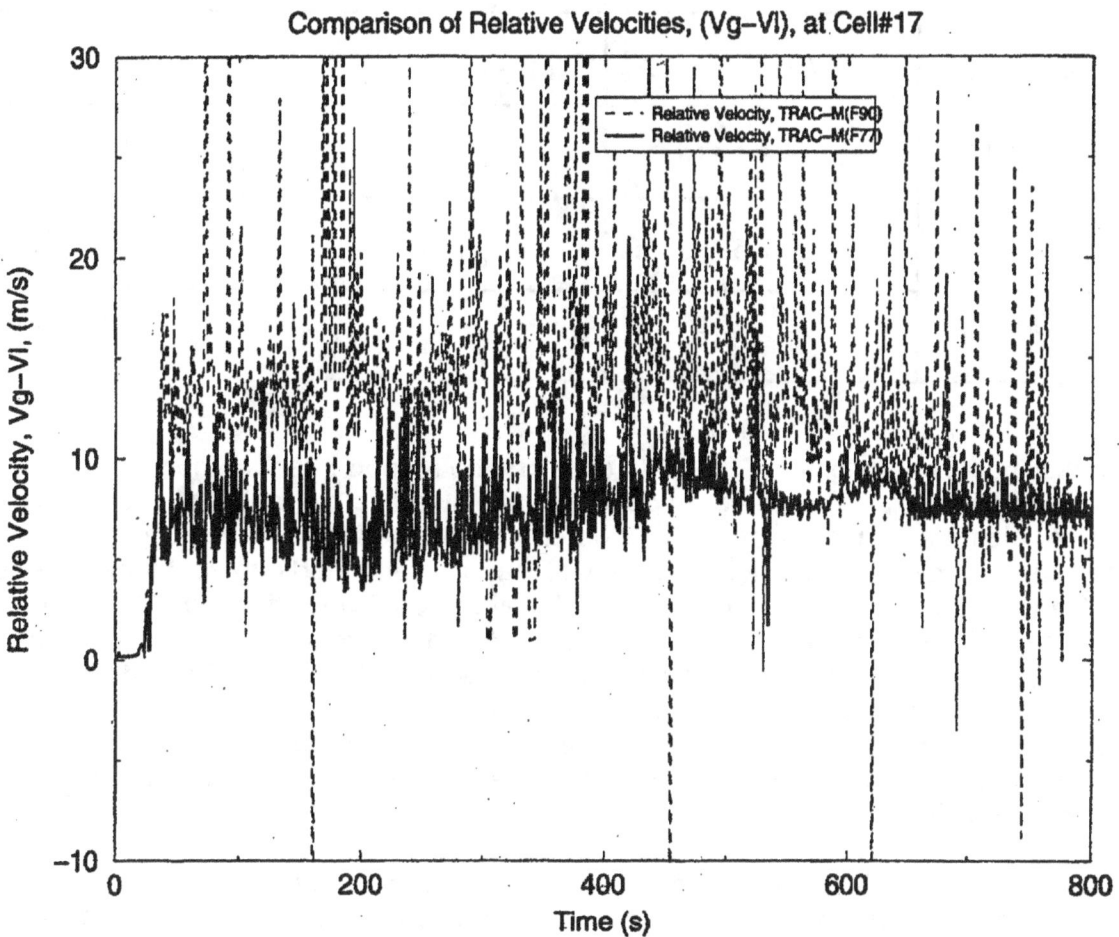

Figure 4.29 Calculated Relative Velocities at Cell #17

TABLE 2

FLOW REGIME TRANSITION CRITERIA

Regime	Ishii's Correlation	Region of Applicability	TRAC Application
Smooth Inverted Annular Flow (IAF)	$Z/D = 60\sqrt{Ca}$	$We/\alpha^2_i \leq 10^{-2}$	$0.05\langle\alpha\langle.3$
Rough Wavy IAF	$Z/D = 295\sqrt{Ca}$	$We/\alpha^2_i \leq 10^{-1}$	$0.3\langle\alpha\langle0.4$
Agitated IAF	$Z/D = 595\sqrt{Ca}$	$We/\alpha^2_i \leq 3.5$	$0.4\langle\alpha\langle0.75$
Dispersed Section	$Z/D = 595\sqrt{Ca}$	$We/\alpha^2_i \leq 10$	$0.75\langle\alpha\langle0.98$

The applicability of correlations in Ref. 16 to simulate the reflood phenomenon during a LOCA may be very limited. Experiments were conducted at a steady state, and flow regimes varied axially. The void fraction in correlations was determined at the inlet of the section, and its value was determined from the test section geometry alone, and remained constant for a given test section. Hence, the break-out lengths depended only on liquid velocities (i.e., Capillary numbers). The region of applicability was determined by the correlations with the Weber number and the void fraction, both of which were evaluated at the inlet of the test section. The break-out lengths did not vary with the amount of power applied to the test section. This can be true only if the amount of heating did not change during tests. Hence, the power or power profile did not enter into correlations. However, in reactor applications, power and power profile can be a major factor.

The TRAC modeling is different in that the Capillary number is calculated using fluid properties at the CHF point. The criteria of applicability of Ishii correlations (i.e., break-out lengths) are predicated on local void fractions. Details of calculations of the local void fractions are presented in Ref. 18. There is no restriction on the basis of the Weber numbers that are calculated using relative velocities.

It is clear that implementation of the flow regime maps modeled by Ishii (Ref. 16) has not been correctly performed in the TRAC code (Refs. 17 and 18). On the other hand, Ishii correlations in Ref. 16 may have important shortcomings in that break-out lengths are independent of the power and power profile of the test section, and correlations are developed using parameters measured at the inlet. They are not local quantities. Determination of the type of reflood modeling in the TRAC code and the type of experiments needed for modeling reflood are outside of the scope of the present assessment.

The Office of Nuclear Regulatory Research has a research program in place at Pennsylvania State University (PSU) to improve the agency's capability to model reflood phenomena using its system analysis codes. The findings in this report provide guidance on how future modeling of reflood should proceed. This report assesses the code against one particular Flecht-Seaset (F-S) run. However, the decision to initiate the PSU test program was based on several reflood cases at various facilities. These cases exhibit the overall trend that TRAC-M(F90) overpredicts peak clad temperature (PCT), even though the predictions are in reasonable agreement with runs made at the CCTF and SCTF facilities. The TRAC-P code series has been used by NRC to perform LOCA analysis because of this conservative trend. However, as the agency begins to risk-inform its regulations, new designs are submitted and licensees request further uprates. NRC would be better equipped to audit licensee submittals with a less conservative, more accurate reflood model. In order to model reflood accurately for all designs, conditions and test facilities, the proper physics must be modeled mechanistically. The author recommends that new flow regime maps for reflood be constructed and the selection criteria for the maps should also include effects of both phasic velocities.

4.5 Sensitivity Calculation without the Choking Model

To evaluate the effect of choking on predictions, a sensitivity study was performed with the TRAC-M(F77) code. The choking model was artificially turned off. Figures. 4.30 through 4.33 compare calculations of the TRAC-M(F77) code with and without the activation of the choking model and those of the TRAC-M(F90) code with the experimental data. As expected, the predictions of the TRAC-M(F77) code without the choking model are very close to those of the TRAC-M(F90) code. There are some small differences, but they are expected because of bug fixes or error corrections in the TRAC-M(F90) code. This comparison shows that the conversion to the TRAC-M(F90) code for this type of application is successful.

4.6 Conclusions

The top-level requirement in the development of a thermal-hydraulic code is that the code should correctly model the physics of the phenomena. This assessment shows that the TRAC code does not correctly model flow regime maps during the reflood and, consequently, it cannot correctly predict interfacial areas between phases, and vapor fractions, phasic velocities, and temperatures. Almost none of the important parameters (such as, clad temperatures, steam temperatures, differential pressures, and liquid and steam carryouts) are consistently predicted throughout the range with acceptable accuracy. The predictions in ranges where clad temperatures are predicted within accuracy limits, are accidental. The predictions of clad temperatures are higher than the experimental data because predictions of liquid carryout by the codes during a reflood have consistently been high. (See also Ref. 15.) Hence, these predictions are conservative.

The comparison of TRAC-M(F77) and TRAC-M(F90) codes and the sensitivity study performed with the TRAC-M(F77) code show that the conversion of the TRAC-M(F77) code to the TRAC-M(F90) code has been successful for this type of application.

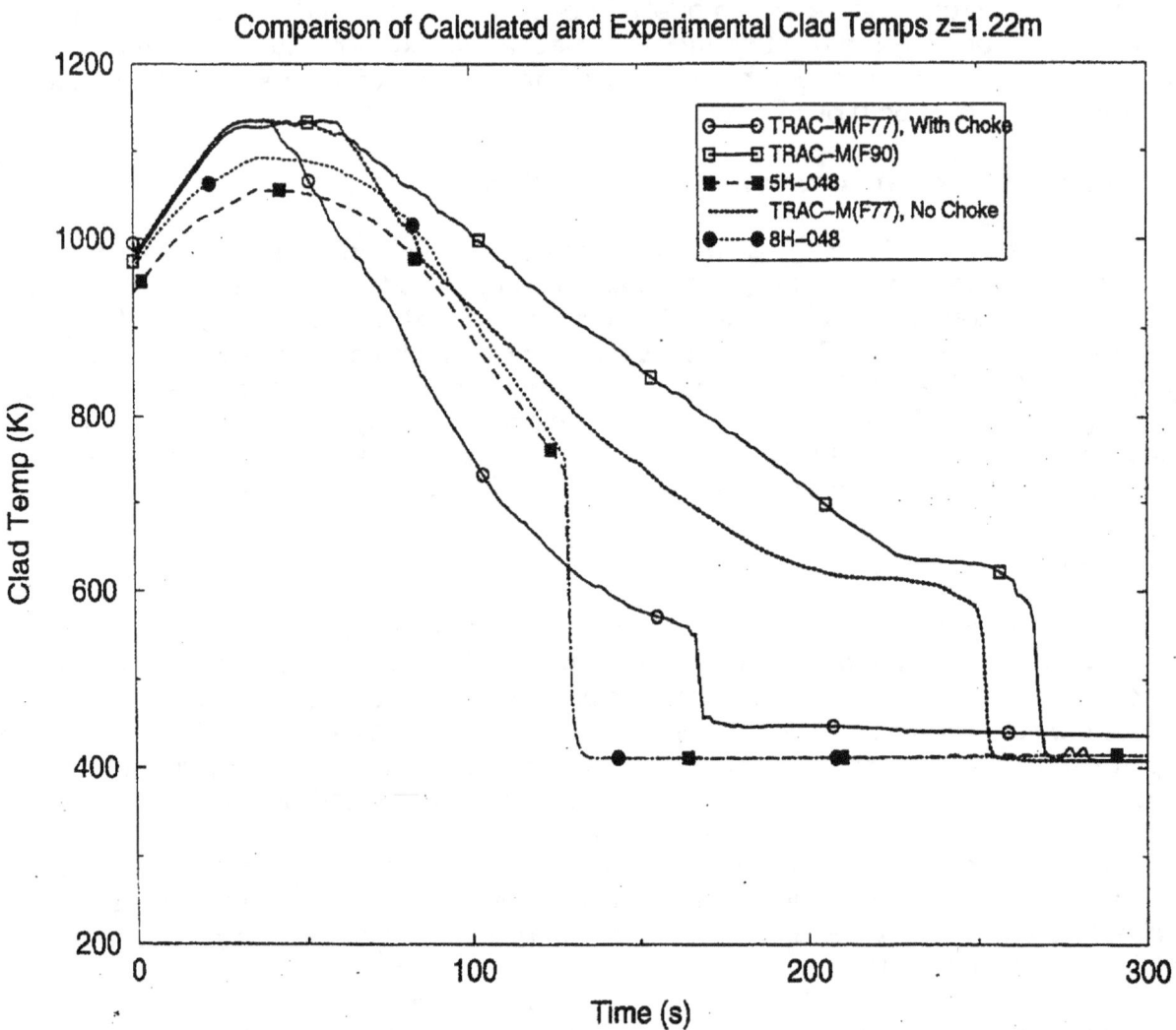

Figure 4.30 Comparison of Clad Temperatures with and without
Choking, Z=1.22m

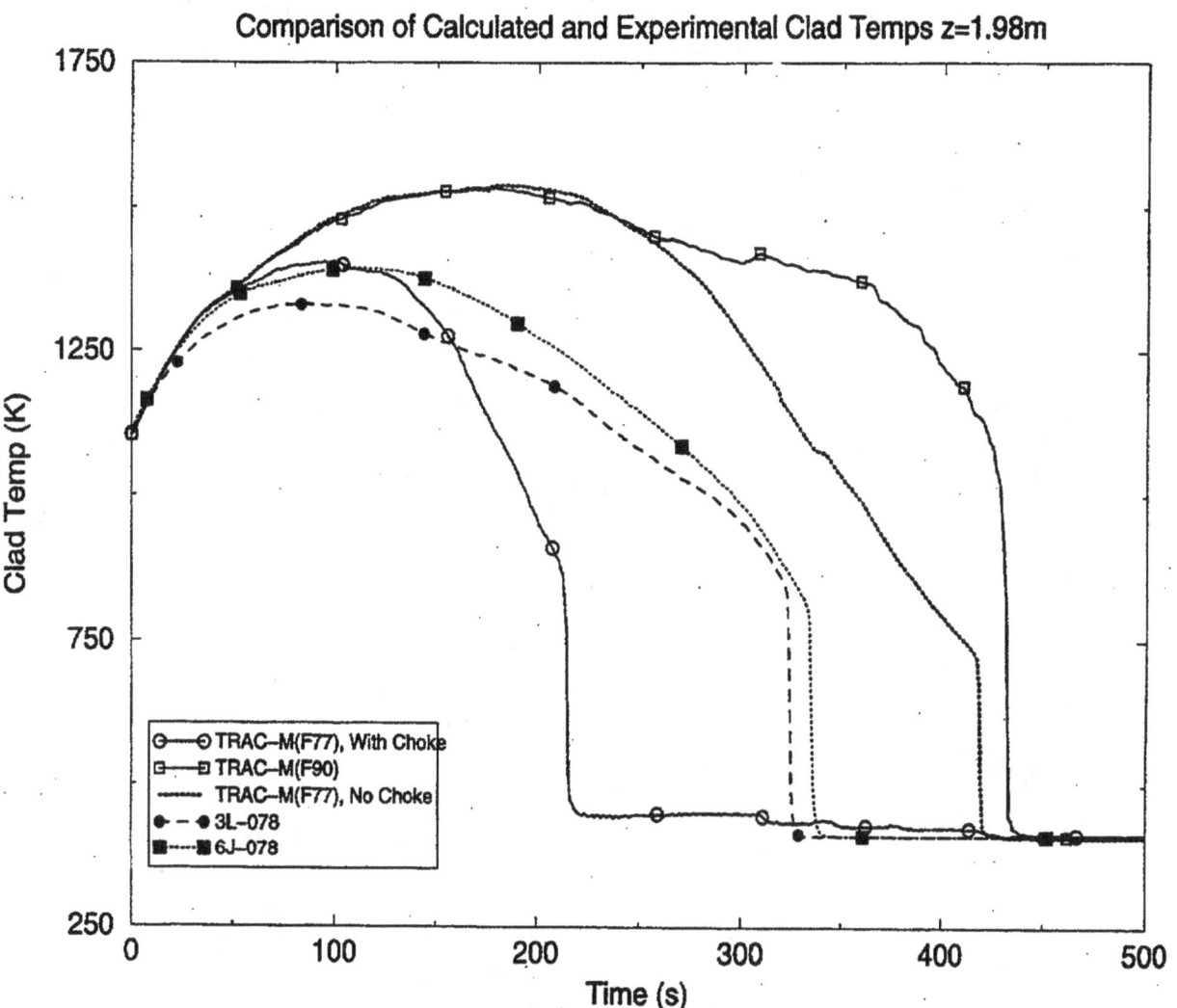

Figure 4.31 Comparison of Clad Temperatures with and without
Choking, Z=1.98m

Flecht–Seaset Forced Reflood 31504

Comparison of Calculated and Experimental Clad Temps z=2.59m

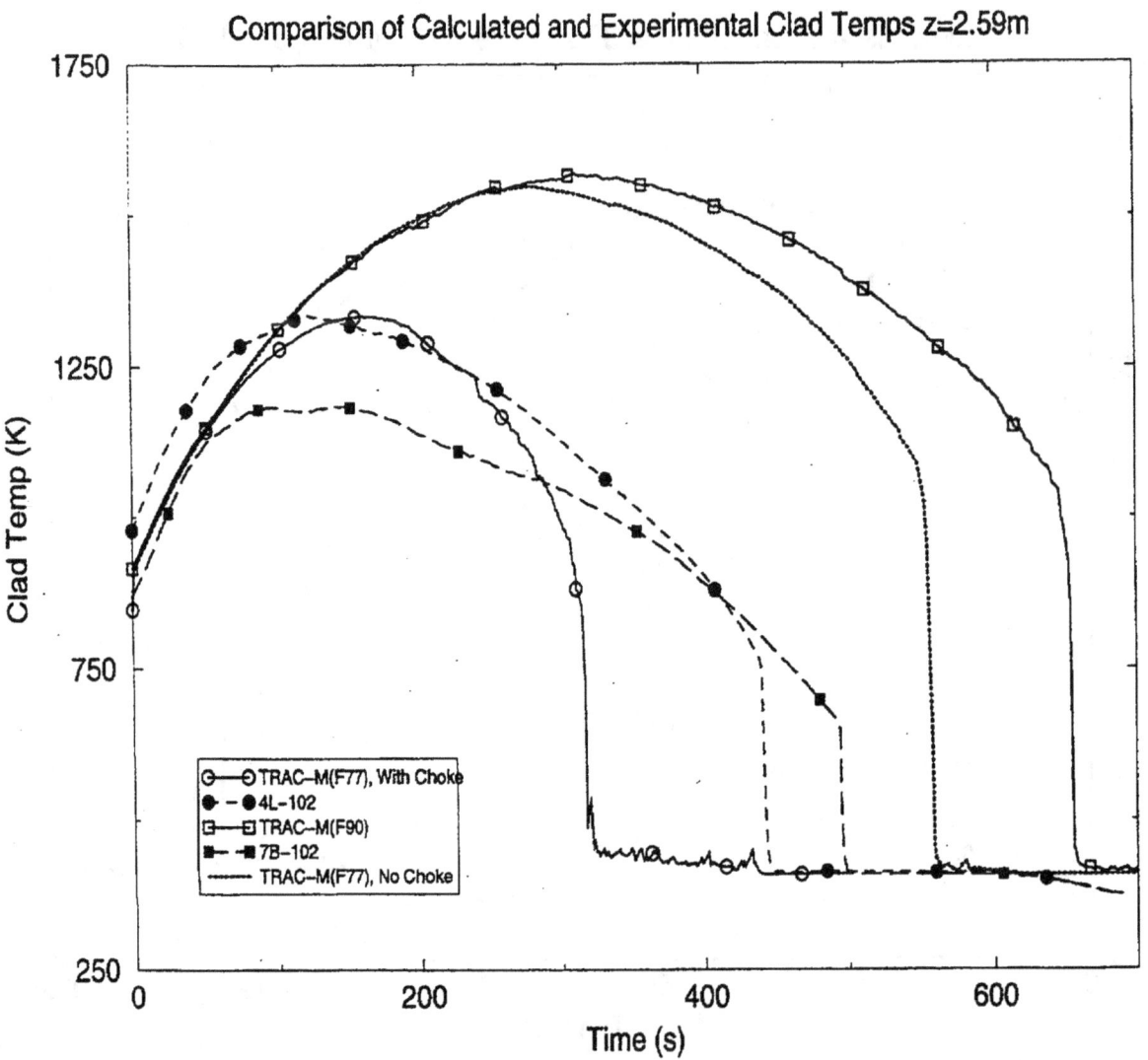

Figure 4.32 Comparison of Clad Temperatures with and without Choking, Z=2.59m

Flecht–Seaset Forced Reflood 31504

Comparison of Calculated and Experimental Clad Temps z=3.35m

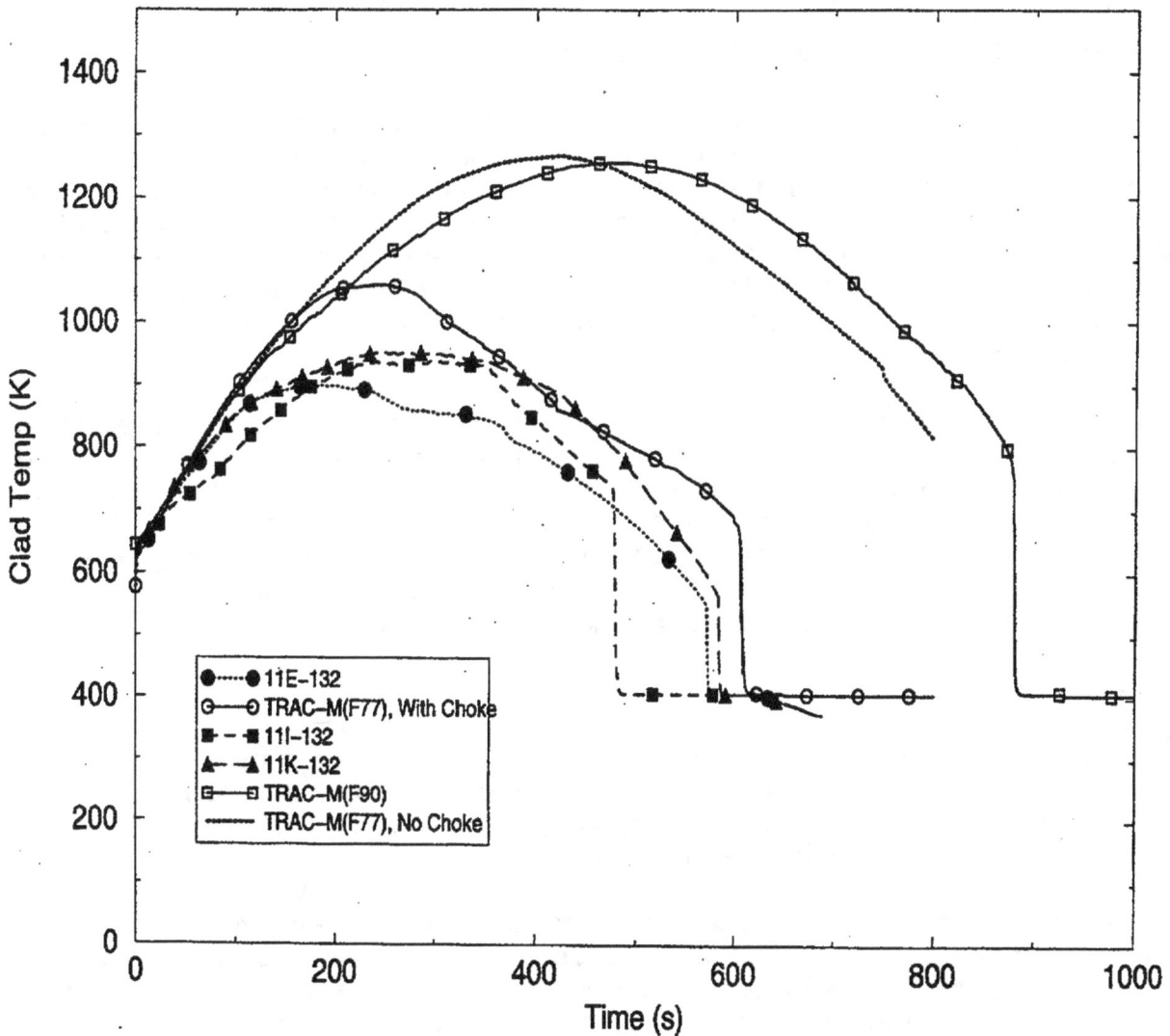

Figure 4.33 Comparison of Clad Temperatures with and without Choking, Z=3.35m

SECTION 5

TRAC-M ASSESSMENT
WITH
FLECHT-SEASET STEAM COOLING TEST DATA, RUN 32753

5.1 Discussion of Phenomena and Code Requirements

The phenomenon that occurs during steam cooling is rather simple. During some part of the transient, the reactor core is assumed to be full of steam, and no liquid is present. The incoming flow from the inlet is also assumed to be steam. The question is whether the incoming steam flow can cool the fuel assemblies. Hence, the capability required from the codes is proper modeling of heat transfer in a convective single-phase flow. The top-level requirement is that codes should model appropriate physics to predict heat transfer in a single-phase flow. The next level of requirements is that trends and important parameters should be predicted with acceptable accuracy.

Steam cooling tests were conducted in the Flecht-Seaset test facility in order to simulate steam cooling conditions in a PWR. These tests were initiated by pressurizing and preheating the rod bundle and associated piping with steam that was slightly superheated. Once the test section was heated above the saturation temperature, the rod power was turned on to a preset value and was kept constant. Tests were run until steady-state conditions were obtained. Hence, the expected primary trend is that clad temperatures will increase and asymptotically approach a steady-state value. The important parameter is the clad temperature.

5.2 Success Metrics

As stated in Section 4.1, validation of thermal-hydraulic codes requires comparison of code predictions with experimental test data. The same definitions will be used for "Qualitative" metrics, as described in Section 4.1 (i.e., "Excellent Agreement," "Reasonable Agreement," "Minimal Agreement," and "Insufficient Agreement").

The quantitative success metric will be determined on the basis of the experimental spread of the clad temperature data, which will be plotted and examined. Figure 5.1 shows the scatter of thermocouple readings at Z=1.52m elevation in Run 32753. The spread of the data is within 70 K, and there is one outlier trace that is giving wrong measurements. This thermocouple trace will not be included in the uncertainty band. The spread is attributed to the natural circulation occurring within the test section because of heat loss from the walls and effects of unheated tubes where steam probes and instruments are located. Locations of unheated rods are shown in Figure 3.2.

If clad temperatures are predicted within 70 K, predictions will be considered "Excellent." It should be noted that data above Z=1.52m elevation were not used for comparisons. Severe rod bundle distortions occurred above this elevation, and a majority of the heater rod temperatures did not attain their steady-state values according to Ref. 19. Because of distortions, many of the runs were not usable.

Flecht–Seaset Steam Cooling Test 32753

Exp. Data, Clad Temps. at z=60in (1.52m)

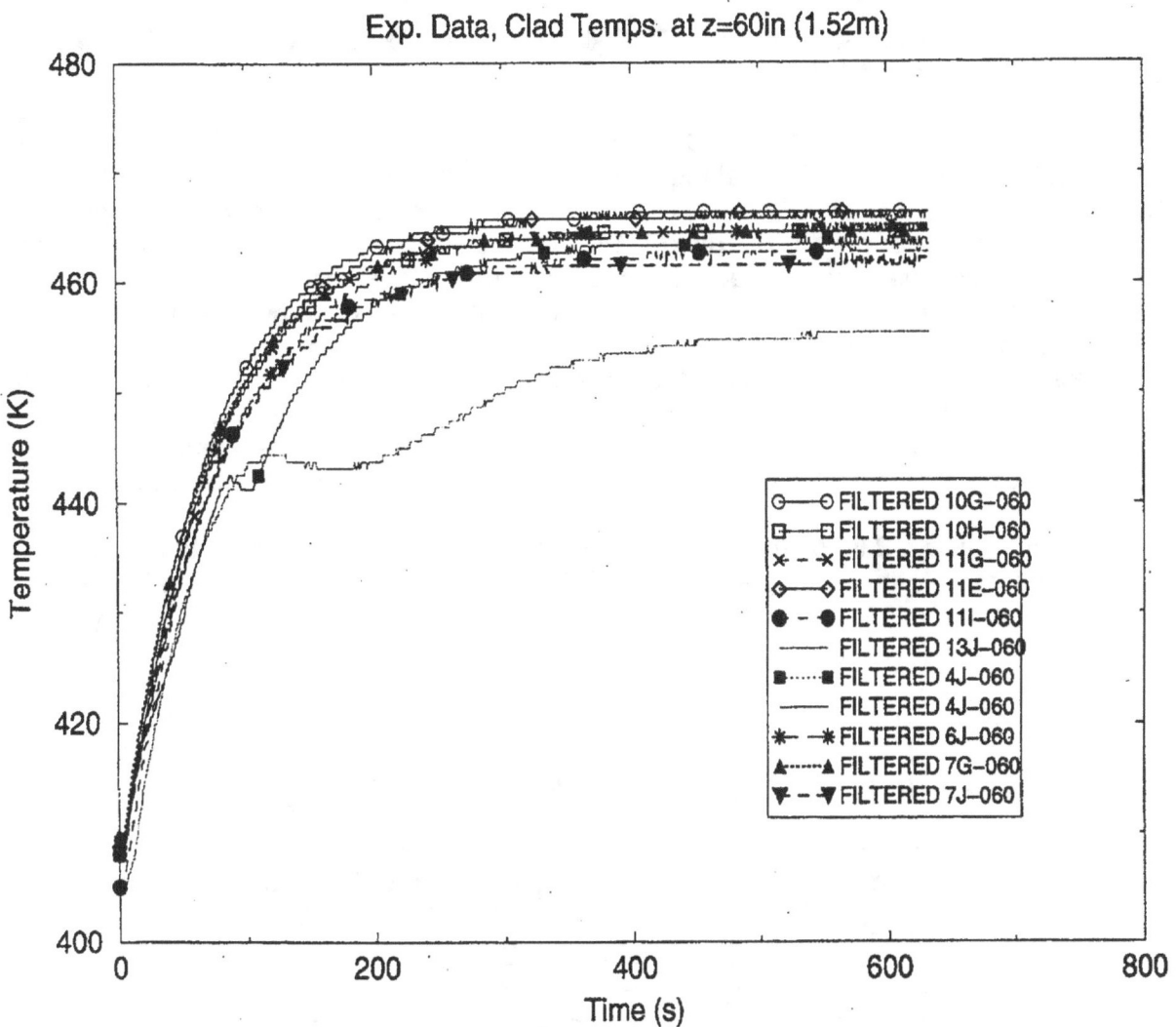

Figure 5.1 Experimental Data, Clad Temperatures at Z=1.52m

5.3 TRAC Input Model for Flecht-Seaset Steam Cooling Run 32753

The TRAC input model schematic used to model steam cooling Flecht-Seaset Run 32753 is similar to the one used Forced Reflood Run 31504, except that the power applied to the test section remained constant with time and the heater rod was finer nodalized than in Run 31504 in order to bring the node interfaces to thermocouple locations for accurate comparisons of code predictions with test data. As in the case of Run 31504, the input deck does not model heat losses from the test section to the environment.

5.4 Comparison of TRAC-M(F77) and TRAC-M(F90) Calculations with Experimental Data from Flecht-Seaset Run 32753

Calculations were performed with TRAC-M(F77) and TRAC-M(F90) codes and compared with experimental data. Table 3 lists initial test conditions for Run 32753. Comparison of predictions by the TRAC-M(F77) and TRAC-M(F90) codes and the test data are presented in Figure 5.2. As stated above, because of severe rod distortions, comparisons are made only up to the elevation of 1.52 m. Comparisons show that agreements between the predictions and the test data at different elevations are well within the uncertainty band of 70 K, up to the elevation of 1.52 m. At this elevation, the differences between code predictions and the thermocouple trace grow to approximately 70 K. The thermocouple trace represents the average of the traces in Figure 5.1. Hence, the agreement is slightly out of the bound of uncertainty, but will be considered "Reasonable" agreement. One reason for this slight difference is that the input deck does not model heat losses from the test section. A slight bias for hotter predictions is expected.

Examination of Figure 5.2 leads to the conclusion that the trend of the test data (i.e., the asymptotic approach to the steady-state values at different elevations) is very well predicted. Code-to-code differences in predictions are approximately null, as expected.

TABLE 3

INITIAL CONDITIONS FOR RUN 32753

Parameter	Test Condition Value
Upper Plenum Pressure	0.28 MPa
Initial Rod Wall Temperature	408 K
Rod Peak Power	0.205 kW/m
Inlet Flow Rate	0.36 kg/sec
Coolant Temperature	405 K
Bundle Radial Profile	Uniform

Flecht–Seaset Steam Cooling Test 32753

Comparison of Clad Temperatures

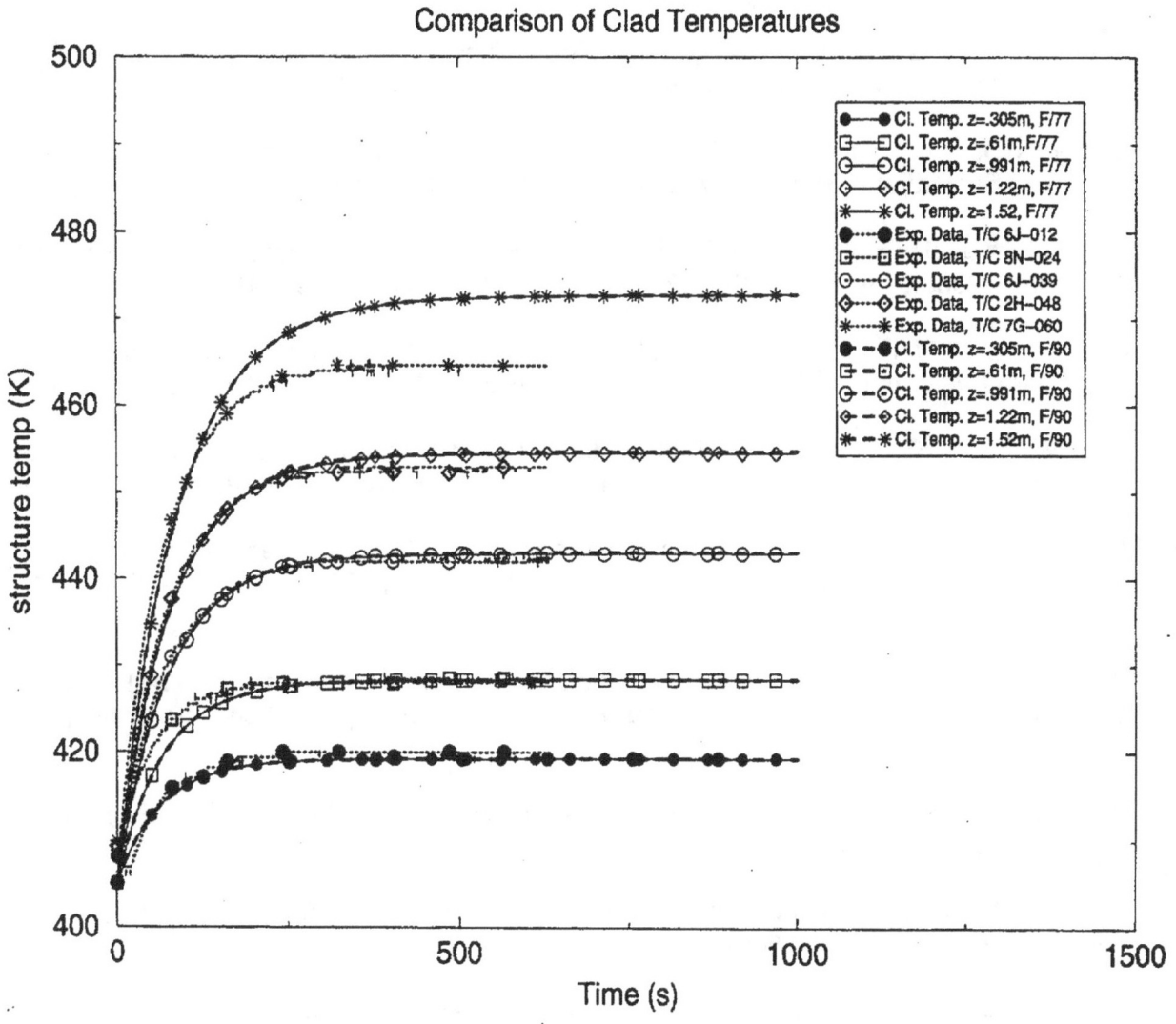

Figure 5.2 Comparison of Predicted and Measured Clad Temperatures

5.5 Conclusions

This assessment shows that both TRAC-M codes correctly predict the single-phase convective flow heat transfer within acceptable accuracy. The agreement between predictions and the test data is "Excellent" to "Reasonable." It is judged that "Excellent" agreement throughout the whole region of valid testing may be obtained by modeling the input deck in more detail.

The comparison of TRAC-M(F77) and TRAC-M(F90) codes show that the conversion of the TRAC-M(F77) code to the TRAC-M(F90) code has been successful for this type of application.

REFERENCES

1. G.G. Loomis and R.W. Shumway, "Transition Boiling Heat Transfer in the Semiscale Mod-3 Core During Reflood," *Nuclear Technology*, "56, 426, March 1982.

2. G. DeJarlais, "An Experimental Study of Inverted Annular Flow Hydrodynamics Utilizing an Adiabatic Simulation," NUREG/CR-3339, ANL-83-44, March 1983.

3. M.J. Loftus et al., "PWR FLECHT-SEASET Unblocked Bundle Forced and Gravity Reflood Task Data Report," NUREG/CR-1532, Vols. 1 and 2, WCAP-9699, 1980.

4. N. Lee et al., "PWR FLECHT-SEASET Unblocked Bundle, Forced and Gravity Reflood Task Data Evaluation and Analysis Report," NUREG/CR-2256, WCAP-9891, 1981.

5. G.E. McCreery, G.G. Loomis, H.R. Bruestle, "Thermal-Hydraulic Analysis of the Semiscale Mod-1 Reflood Test Series (Gravity Feed Tests)," TREE-NUREG-1010, Jan., 1977.

6. A.C. Peterson, G.G. Loomis, L.L. Chen, "Thermal and Hydraulic Response of the Semiscale Mod1 Core During Forced Feed Reflood Tests," TREE-NUREG-1001, Oct., 1976.

7. R. Deruz and J.M. Veteau, "Pericles Reflood Experiments," presented at *11th Water Reactor Safety Information Meeting*, Gaithersburg, MD, 1983, NUREG/CP-0048, Vols. 1–6, January 1984.

8. P. Ihle and L. Rust, "FEBA-Flooding Experiments with Blocked Arrays, Data Report 1, Test Series I through IV," KfK 3658, March 1984.

9. P. Ihle and L. Rust, "FEBA-Flooding Experiments with Blocked Arrays, Data Report 2, Test Series V through VIII," KfK 3649, March 1984.

10. K. G. Pearson et al., "Reflooding Experiments on a 49-Rod Containing a Long 90% Blockage, AEEW-R-1591, January 1983.

11. V.J. Dhir and M. Fruckler, "Studies of a Single and Two-Phase Heat Transfer in a Blocked 4-Rod Bundle," EPRI Report NP-3485, June 1984.

12. S.L. Lee, S.K. Cho, H.J. Sheen, "Reentrainment of Droplets from Grid Spacers in Mist Flow Portion of a LOCA Reflood of a PWR," *NRC/ANS Topical Meeting on Basic Thermal-Hydraulic Mechanisms in LWR Analysis*, September 1982, NUREG/CP-0043, 1983.

13. Seban et al., "UC-B Reflood Program: Experimental Data Report," EPRI/NP-743, April 1978.

14. Y. Murao et al., "Experimental and Analytical Modeling of the Reflood Phase During PWR LOCA," paper presented at the *19th National Heat Transfer Conference*, Orlando, Florida (ASME), July 27-30, 1980.

15. B.E. Boyack, J.F. Lime, D.A. Pimentel, J.W. Spore, and J.L. Steiner, "TRAC-M:FORTRAN 77, Version 5.5, Developmental Assessment Manual, Volume I: Nonproprietary Assessment Sections," LA-UR-99-6480, December 1999.

16. N.T. Obot and M. Ishii, "Two Phase Flow Regime Transition Criteria in Post-Dryout Region Based on Flow Visualization Experiments," *Int. J. Heat Mass Transfer,* Vol. 31, No.12, pp 2559–2570, 1988.

17. R.A. Nelson, D.A. Pimentel, S.J. Jolly-Woodruff, and J.W. Spore, "A Phenomenological Thermal-Hydraulic Model of Hot Rod Bundles Experiencing Simultaneous Bottom and Top Quenching and Optimization Methodology for Closure Development," LA-UR-98-3043, April 1998.

18. J.W. Spore, J.S. Elson, S.J. Jolly-Woodruff, T.D. Knight, J.C. Lin, R.A. Nelson, K.O. Pasamehmetoglu, R.G. Steinke, and C. Unal of Los Alamos National Laboratory and J.H. Mahaffy and C. Murray of Pennsylvania State University, "TRAC-M/FORTRAN 90 (Version 3.0), Theory Manual," LA-UR-00-910, March 2000.

19. S. Wong and L.E. Hochreiter, "Analysis of Flecht-Seaset Unblocked Bundle Steam Cooling and Boiloff Tests," NUREG/CR-1533, January 1981.

NRC FORM 335 (2-89) NRCM 1102, 3201, 3202	U.S. NUCLEAR REGULATORY COMMISSION	1. REPORT NUMBER (Assigned by NRC, Add Vol., Supp., Rev., and Addendum Numbers, if any.)
	BIBLIOGRAPHIC DATA SHEET (See instructions on the reverse)	NUREG-1744

2. TITLE AND SUBTITLE

Assessment of TRAC-M Codes Using Flecht-Seaset Reflood and Steam Cooling Data

3.	DATE REPORT PUBLISHED	
	MONTH	YEAR
	May	2001

4. FIN OR GRANT NUMBER

5. AUTHOR(S)

F. Odar

6. TYPE OF REPORT

Technical

7. PERIOD COVERED *(Inclusive Dates)*

8. PERFORMING ORGANIZATION - NAME AND ADDRESS *(If NRC, provide Division, Office or Region, U.S. Nuclear Regulatory Commission, and mailing address; if contractor, provide name and mailing address.)*

Division of System Analysis and Regulatory Effectiveness

Office of Nuclear Regulatory Research

U.S. Nuclear Regulatory Commission

Washington, DC 20555-0001

9. SPONSORING ORGANIZATION - NAME AND ADDRESS *(If NRC, type "Same as above"; if contractor, provide NRC Division, Office or Region, U.S. Nuclear Regulatory Commission, and mailing address.)*

Same as 8. Above.

10. SUPPLEMENTARY NOTES

11. ABSTRACT *(200 words or less)*

This report presents the results of an assessment work performed using TRAC-M(F 77), Version 5.5.2A and TRAC-M(F90), Version 3.580 codes. The report assesses capabilities of both codes to predict reflood and steam cooling phenomena which may occur during a postulated Large Break Loss of Coolant Accident, LBLOCA. The assessment is based on Flecht-Seaset Run 31504 and 32753 test data. The assessment shows that both codes' predictions of the reflood phenomena are not accurate; however, it is judged that they conservatively predict peak clad temperatures in heated rods since the model expels more water from the test section than measured. The predictions of steam cooling in single phase flow conditions are acceptable.

12. KEY WORDS/DESCRIPTORS *(List words or phrases that will assist researchers in locating the report.)*

Reflood
Steam Cooling
Thermal Hydraulics
Computer Codes
Code Assessment
Code Validation

13. AVAILABILITY STATEMENT

unlimited

14. SECURITY CLASSIFICATION

(This Page)

unclassified

(This Report)

unclassified

15. NUMBER OF PAGES

16. PRICE

This form was electronically produced by Elite Federal Forms, Inc.

Federal Recycling Program

UNITED STATES
NUCLEAR REGULATORY COMMISSION
WASHINGTON, DC 20555-0001

OFFICIAL BUSINESS
PENALTY FOR PRIVATE USE, $300

www.ingramcontent.com/pod-product-compliance
Lightning Source LLC
Chambersburg PA
CBHW081841280526
45789CB00007B/2529

* 9 7 8 1 4 9 9 6 4 4 3 1 9 *